$3.95

The cost of this book is Deductible!

This book is dedicated to the "little guys" who can not afford those "extra" tax dollars they unnecessarily contribute to the federal government each year.

To those who have always backed away from doing their own taxes because of the complicated language and the "exotic" math involved.

To those who are willing to spend a few hours studying the examples in this book which will pay for themselves ten times over.

To those who really need to save money this year.

And especially to my wife, Judy, whose confidence in me never wavered.

Tax Loopholes
for the Little Guy

Jim Donaldson

OLIVER PRESS
Willits, California

Library of Congress Card Number 76-43184
ISBN 0-914400-31-2

Cover by Lynn Braswell

First Printing January, 1977

OLIVER PRESS
1400 Ryan Creek Road
Willits, California 95490

Introduction

When most people hear the words "tax loopholes" they usually think of the large corporations with their batteries of lawyers taking advantage of the various means available to save millions of dollars per year in tax money.

Just a few examples should serve to illustrate how flagrant this abuse is.

Mrs. Horace Dodge, heir to the Dodge automobile millions, was able, before her timely death in 1970, at age 103, to amass over 100 million dollars worth of municipal bonds, state indebtedness notes, and similar tax free securities. These securities had put her in a position of being able to realize an annual income of over 5 million dollars. Not only did she reap this monstrous income, but, since these investments were all tax free securities, she did not even have to bother filing an income tax return. All this was accomplished by and with the aid of one loophole: tax free investments.

Now let us see what one enterprising gentleman did by taking advantage of some of the other tax loopholes available to those who have the time or money (all you need is the price of this book) to search them out.

Robert Short, the trucking millionaire, decided, for reasons that will soon be obvious, to purchase the Washington Senators baseball team. Actually, he purchased 90% interest for a reported purchase price of 9 million dollars. Now Mr. Short did not become a millionaire by throwing away handfulls of dollars into baseball teams: especially none whose won/lost record was almost as bad as their profit/loss statement. What

Mr. Short actually did was put up $1,000.00 hard cash. "The rest of the purchase price was made up of loans, some of them guaranteed by Short, and by the issue of preferred stock." **The Washington Post** of Dec. 19, 1971 from which the previous quote was taken goes on to state "Short vigorously refrained from pouring his own cash into the team—except as a loan, in the purchase, from one of his own companies, at a 9.75% interest rate." This amazing bit of juggling made Mr. Short and/or his companies eligible for tax reductions of over 4 million dollars during the next several years. In just the year 1970 he was eligible to realize "over half a million dollars in tax reductions." This was due largely to a loophole called "player depreciation," which, of course, is awarded to the club owner rather than the player, who is the one suffering from the loss of earning potential. Finally, in 1971, Mr. Short decided that he had suffered enough, and petitioned the American League; citing his huge losses (but not mentioning his huge tax savings), and won permission to move the club to Texas.

What most people don't realize, however, is that the "little guy" also has tax loopholes he can use. He can cut his tax bill drastically by the use of such loopholes as rental property, profit sharing, automobile expense, health plans, tax shelters and more.

Who fits into this "little guy" category? There is the small businessman. He may own a grocery store, service station, liquor store, or any other business. There is the middle income salesman or bank officer. There are the farmers, skilled and unskilled laborers, bartenders, ministers and countless other people who have long been paying too much tax while big business routinely slipped through the legal loopholes.

In 1895, while arguing the constitutionality of income tax before the Supreme Court, Attorney James C. Carter said:

"In every community those who feel the burden of taxation are naturally prone to relieve themselves if they can . . . One class struggles to throw the burden off its own shoulders. If they succeed, of course, it must fall upon others. They also, in their turn, labor to get rid of it, and finally the load falls upon those who will not, or cannot, make a successful effort for relief.''

He also said:

"This is, in general, a one-sided struggle, in which the rich **only** engage and . . . in which the poor always go to the wall.''

But is this necessary? Must the poor always carry the burden of the rich man's evasions?

What are tax loopholes? To many people this term implies something illegal. Not so! These loopholes are written into the tax laws to make allowances for such things as business expenses, long term investments, care of dependents and various business losses. Every taxpayer should know about these loopholes and how to use them to his best advantage.

Here, at last, is a book which explains to the little guy the many means available to him to legally lessen much of his tax burden. This is not an attempt to get him to avoid his duties as a citizen but rather to give him the same advantage held by those more able to pay tax attorneys.

CONT

E N T S

1976 Tax Law Changes

A parent who does not have custody of a child/children may now claim an exemption for each child if he contributes at least $1200.00 for each child, and the parent having custody can't show that he/she contributed more. This change is effective in 1977. 1976 law reads a $1200.00 contribution for all children.

As of 1976 you can no longer claim exclusion for sick pay, unless you are retiring under age 65, or are totally and permanently disabled on retiring: then he/she may claim as much as $100.00 per week of disability pension exclusion. This is reduced when the taxpayer has an adjusted gross income of over $15,000.00.

In 1976 the minimum mileage you could move and still deduct all or part of your moving expense was 50 miles. This is reduced to 35 miles in 1977. Also, after 1976 the deduction for: expenses due to sale, purchase, or lease of home, house hunting, and temporary living expenses increased to $500.00 from $2500.00 to $3000.00. No more than $1500.00 of this may be charged against pre-move house hunting and/or temporary living quarters.

Mutual fund dividends. The Tax Reform Act of 1976 also states that the part or whole of a mutual funds receipt of tax exempt interest is not taxable to the individual shareholder. This is indeed a break for the little guy; who can now invest in a mutual fund specializing in tax exempt securities and receive the same type of exemption that the big tax exempt holders now enjoy.

Those using their homes as offices should be aware of the tax rule changes effective as of 1976. If you use your home as an office you may deduct only that part of the home used exclusively and regularly as your main place of business, or as a place where you carry on business with patients, clients, or customers. Also this home office expense may not be greater than the income generated by those home business activities. Be careful because you may not use that business portion of your home for any personal purposes.

If you have a net operating loss to carry over, the new laws state that you may now extend this carry over loss for seven years instead of five. Also you may forego the carry back provision and elect to simply carry forward the loss for seven years.

For security options written after September 1, 1976, principals realize short-term capital gain/loss on closing transactions, and short-term capital gain on lapses. Options issued before September 2, 1976, are subject to ordinary profit/loss treatment.

After 1976, the period you must hold an investment for it to be considered a long-term capital gain is increased from 6 months to 9 months in 1977, and to 1 year in 1978. The exception to this is commodity or farm futures which continue to be long-term capital gains after 6 months.

There is also a new set of rules governing inherited property, but they are so complicated that a good accountant or tax lawyer is needed for their interpretation.

For capital losses sustained in 1976 the deduction remains at $1000.00, but in 1977 this deduction is increased to $2000.00, and in 1978 to $3000.00.

There is also a revision in the bad debt rule. It states that business bad debts are now limited to debts arising directly from the guarantor's business. Other bad debts must now be treated as non-business bad debts, and are deductible as short-term capital losses.

No one is likely to complain about tax cuts. The 1976 rules have included many new cuts over 1975. The IRS now allows a $35.00 tax credit per dependency exemption (or 2% of the first $9000.00 of taxable income, which ever is more). This compares to $30.00 exemption in 1975. There is also an increase in standard deductions. The maximum has been raised to $2,800.00 for joint returns and $2,400.00 for singles. Minimums are $2100.00 and $1700.00 respectively. These deductions are for those who do not itemize their returns.

Heads of household can benefit from the new tax laws. Those with less than $8000.00 earned income may deduct up to $400.00 from their taxes. One is eligible if he maintains a household for himself and one or more dependents under age 19 or a full time student. Married heads of household must file a joint return.

Employees who receive company stock as part of their pay must now pay tax on the difference between the option price and the fair market value of the stock. If the employee receives the stock at $5 per share and the stock is sold to the public at $10 per share, the difference of $5 will be taxable as income.

Many people maintain vacation homes and rent them out part of the year thus enabling themselves to deduct several maintenance costs. The new law says that the owner may not use the home more than 14 days or 10% of the rental time. Otherwise the deductions are allowable only for the time the home was rented.

The IRS has increased the amount of taxes which must be paid by American citizens working outside the country. The amount of taxable income has been reduced from $20,000 to $15,000 and no longer is credit allowed for foreign taxes paid.

As of 1977 there is now a provision allowing an IRA (Individual Retirement Account) for a non-working spouse. The working spouse may contribute 15% of his income up to $1750.00 to a joint IRA account, or up to $875.00 each in separate IRA accounts.

Of news to the farmer, is a change covering disaster relief payments. The cash basis farmer receiving this type of insurance payment may now elect to report the insurance in the year after the year of damage on payments received after December 31, 1973. Sales of livestock necessitated by drought are also subject to this year-after type of option.

Realtors, builders and investors should know of a change in the handling of construction time interest and real estate taxes during this period. A ten year amortization period is going into effect and its application depends largely on the type of building being constructed.

If you have a student government loan cancelled due to working in certain geographical areas; (such as a low income area,) that cancelled part of the loan is non-taxable. The cancellation must be in accordance with the original terms of the loan, and it must be cancelled before January 1, 1979.

Prepaid interest is now subject to a new law which states that this interest must be deducted over the period of the loan, and that you may not deduct any portion of that interest that falls outside the current taxable year.

As of January 1, 1977 you will be allowed to deduct alimony payments from your gross income and still claim the standard deduction.

If your income is under $20,000.00 you must use the tax table supplied for standard deductions. This new tax table replaces the optional tables that were used in previous years.

The new credit for the elderly, which replaces the retirement income credit, has increased the deduction available to those not receiving Social Security or Railroad Retirement to a maximum of $375.00 for a single person or $562.50 for a married couple.

In claiming carryovers and carrybacks for investment credit the new law states that credits carried over from previous years must be used first. After that, currently earned credits are applied. Carryback credits are then applied last.

In 1977 an employer may provide tax-free benefits under a qualified group legal services plan. This plan could provide you and your family with personal prepaid legal services and advice.

One final change requires preparers of income tax to sign the returns they prepare. If they do not they are subject to penalties, including a $25.00 fine.

GETTYSBURG ADDRESS: MODERN VERSION

Five score and fourteen years ago our fathers brought forth upon this nation a new tax, conceived in desperation and dedicated to the proposition that all men are fair game. Now we are engaged in a great mass of calculations, testing whether this taxpayer or any taxpayer so confused and so impoverished can long endure.

We are met on Form 1040. We have come to dedicate a large portion of our income to a final resting place with those men who here spend their lives that they may spend our money. It is altogether anguish and torture that we do this. But in a larger sense, we cannot evade, we cannot cheat, we cannot under-estimate this tax. The collectors, clever and sly, who computed here, have gone far beyond our poor power to add and subtract.

Our creditors will little note nor long remember what we pay here, but the Bureau of Internal Revenue can never forget what we report here.

It is not for us, the taxpayers, to question the tax which the government has thus far so nobly spent. It is rather for us to be here dedicated to the great task remaining before us — that from these vanishing dollars we take increased devotion to the few remaining; that we here highly resolve that next year will not find us in a higher income bracket; that this taxpayer, underpaid, shall figure out more deductions; and that this tax of the people, by the Congress, for the government, shall not cause solvency to perish.

— Author Unknown

Chapter 1

Why Do We Let It Happen?

A history of the "Dragon At Your Doorstep." Why and how the IRS was founded. How it has grown, and changes in its structure. The basic philosophy of finding and using legal "loopholes" to ease your tax burden. How not to feel quite so intimidated by the IRS's "intimidation" techniques and philosophy. Preparing yourself to take full advantage of these "tax breaks" that are written into our tax laws, and realizing that they are also available for you, "the little guy," and not just for the corporate giants. Think savings.

What is this monster named IRS—this overpowering government agency that causes strong men to shake with fear and loathing at any confrontation with it? The Internal Revenue Service has been with us since the earliest days of our nation. The Founding Fathers recognized that our government needed to raise money from sources within the country, as well as from import and export duties. The cost of government was such that those external sources were simply not enough.

In the beginning, our internal revenue was derived primarily from excise taxes, gift taxes, estate taxes, taxes

1

on liquor and tobacco, and others. There was no tax charged on income until the tremendous expenses of the Civil War created a need for more money. Congress, in its wisdom, passed a bill establishing a Commissioner of Internal Revenue, and it was signed into law by President Abraham Lincoln, on July 1, 1862. A note of historical interest is that President Lincoln, on that same day, also signed a law making polygamy a crime.

This first income tax, brought about by the necessity of financing the war between the states, lasted for only ten years. It was repealed by Congress in 1872, after they found that an income tax during peacetime was unnecessary. The Income Tax Division of the Internal Revenue Service was abandoned.

In 1894, Congress once again attempted to levy an income tax on the people. An amendment to the Wilson-Gorman Tariff Act called for a tax of two percent on incomes over $4,000.00 per year. The Internal Revenue Service reorganized their Income Tax Division over many protests from members of the Congress.

However, the Supreme Court ruled this new income tax to be unconstitutional. The Income Tax Division was put back on the shelf before it could collect a dollar.

The government's need for more income was becoming greater and greater. And the time's they were a'changin'. In 1909, Congress ordered the Internal Revenue Service to collect a one percent excise tax on corporation profits above $5,000.00. This thinly disguised income tax apparently escaped the scrutiny of the Supreme Court. At any rate, the tax remained.

President William Howard Taft urged members of Congress to amend the Constitution of the United States to give the government the power to tax incomes. The Sixteenth Amendment to the Constitution was passed by Congress, and ratified by forty-two of the then forty-eight states in 1913. The chief sponsors of the amendment were the Republicans, who through political misjudgement, assumed that it would not be ratified by the states. Secretly, the Republicans were against the amendment, but they lost this political gamble.

The initial tax rate was set at 1% on personal income up to $20,000.00 (income less than $3,000.00 was not taxed at all). Above $20,000.00, the rate progressed up to a whopping 6% maximum. This rate schedule was short-lived. In four short years, World War I brought about a drastic escalation of the tax rates, from 1% to 6% for lower-income people, and from 6% to 77% at the maximum.

These emergency rates were reduced after the war. The low end of the scale was brought back almost to its pre-war level, and the maximum tax was reduced to 25%.

Then came the Depression, and with it greatly lowered incomes and, naturally, greatly lower tax revenue. Franklin Roosevelt and the New Deal changed all that. With government revenue drastically reduced, and the apparent need for government spending to put people back to work, taxes were steadily increased during this period.

World War II brought about dramatic increases in income tax, as well as other taxes. The tax rate scale at that time ranged from 19% to 88%, and an emergency tax of 5% on all but the lowest earners, was tacked on top of the normal income tax. This was the so-called "Victory Tax." Excise taxes on such items as gasoline, tobacco, liquor, jewelry, furs, telephone calls, and travel were also increased substantially at this time.

The tax reduction that had followed our wars in the past didn't come this time. Congress passed some minor tax reduction bills, but our involvement in the Korean War offset these in short order.

After Korea, when we might have expected a tax reduction, we moved directly into the "Cold War," and enormous government spending programs, both in defense and in domestic affairs, were sustained.

Since the Viet Nam War, our taxes have been reduced somewhat. In 1977, the tax rate will range from 14% to 70% for individuals. Corporations pay 22% on the first $25,000.00 of net earnings, with a 26% surtax on earnings in excess of $25,000.00. In other words, the maximum tax for corporations is 48%, and that rate only applies to net

3

earnings over $25,000.00.

From the time of the first income tax in 1862, the Internal Revenue Service has been growing. In fact, within six months of the establishment of IRS, it had grown to be a bureau of more than four thousand men. At that time, the Internal Revenue Service, under the direction of Joseph J. Lewis, made the first moves in the direction of their audit function, instead of being simply tax collectors.

One directive of Commissioner Lewis stated, "Let Assistant Tax Assessors understand that it is their business . . . to ascertain whether they (the tax returns) are correct." In addition to his own staff of "auditors," Lewis also hired private tax collectors, paying them a bounty of 50% of what they collected.

Through the ups and downs of the Internal Revenue Service, it has grown so that now nearly 65,000 people are employed by this giant bureau. And the "bounty hunter" precedent set by Joseph J. Lewis still lives, in the form of a "Reward for Original Information" for tips that result in the collection of delinquent taxes.

Any person who wishes to do so, may inform the Internal Revenue Service that he or she suspects another individual of tax dodging. The informant has nothing to lose. If the lead is erroneous, the informers are not held accountable for any investigation leading from their tip. If the tipster is correct, the reward can be anywhere from 1% to 10% of the delinquent tax collected.

Also, many Internal Revenue Service Auditors approach their job with an attitude of unspoken threat. They wear smug little smiles when speaking to taxpayers, and frequently ignore questions that are asked, for the single purpose of intimidation. In fairness to the Auditors of the Internal Revenue Service, the vast majority of them are fair and conscientious. Most of them are not interested in "intimidation," but only in arriving at the truth. They are honestly not concerned whether or not their audit results in additional cost to the taxpayer. But they suffer the sins of the few who enjoy watching a taxpayer crawl.

Intimidation is what causes the fear in us when it comes to discussion of the Internal Revenue Service. It is a three-pronged fork: First, the attitude of the few offending auditors is remembered by the taxpayer far more strongly than that of the "good guys;" Second, the "bounty hunter" system, funded by an unpublicized appropriation from Congress in excess of $500,000 each year, makes us aware that even a completely unfounded tip could cause us substantial loss of income, as well as grief and discomfort; and Third, the enormous size of the Internal Revenue Service, along with their "all knowing" computer, holds most of us in awe.

It is this size and sometimes lack of response that is perhaps the most frustrating thing about IRS. They have a policy that any question regarding a taxpayer's return, must be channelled through a central office, which has a direct hookup with the computer. Unfortunately, in many cases, any phone calls to these offices must go through a "toll free" telephone number.

Now, on the surface of it, this seems like the Internal Revenue Service is offering us a good deal . . . we can phone them at any time and not have to pay for the call. But like most "good deals" from the government, this one has a catch. It is next to impossible to get them to answer the phone. And when they do answer, most often all you get is a recording telling you that someone will be with you as soon as they are available.

You ought to try it sometime. If you are connected with a real, live person in less than one-half hour, you can feel that you have received exceptional service. Apparently, during the "tax season," they have far more people working in these offices to handle the increased flow of taxpayer questions. This seems logical until you realize that they seem to lag somewhat behind the demand. And during the "off season," all these extra people are laid off, since far fewer people call then. At any rate, an attempted phone call on one of these toll-free numbers is an exercise in futility.

This is just one example of the unresponsiveness of the Internal Revenue Service. Another, more common, example is the tax booklet that each taxpayer receives every year. This booklet is supposed to tell the taxpayer how to fill out the required forms and how to calculate his tax. It does a pretty fair job of telling us about **how to pay**, but it misses the mark widely when telling us how to avoid paying more than we should. For the most part, the information is there, but it is frequently sketchy, or clouded in legalese, so that it is of little use. And when you consider the thumb of intimidation that we are under, it is not surprising that many people overpay their taxes.

How many times have you wondered about the deductibility of an expense, unable to find a specific answer in your tax booklet? How often have you **not** claimed a deductible expense because you did not have a receipt? And how often have you understated an expense because you felt that it would cause you problems with the Internal Revenue Service?

If any of these situations have come up during your tax preparation, the chances are pretty good that you "played it safe," and did not take full advantage of your deductions. And if that is the case, you are not an exception. Most taxpayers, if they are left to act on their own, will feel the fear and loathing for the Internal Revenue Service; and having felt it, they will decide to keep a low profile.

A case in point is a good friend of mine. Bill Brown is a successful, young executive for a small corporation. He once told me that he always took the standard deduction because he did not wish to be audited, even though by doing so he sometimes overpaid his taxes by as much as $500.00. He was very obviously intimidated by IRS. I am happy to report that he has overcome his fear of this omnipotent government agency, and that he now takes every possible advantage of his deductions.

The proper way to approach your income tax problem is to keep this thought always in mind: The law says that each of us must pay taxes to maintain our government, and regardless of how we might feel about the way our tax money is spent, we would be in violation of the law if we cheat. HOWEVER, that does not mean that we should not make the laws work to our advantage.

The rich and powerful people who exert influence in the halls of Congress, and who benefit most from the loopholes that seem to be written in most of our tax laws, have known this all along.

The following chapters hopefully will help you overcome some of your fear of the Internal Revenue Service. They will show many ways to minimize your tax burden, ALL LEGAL. They will demonstrate how different investments fit different people and situations.

One thing they will not do! They will not show you how to cheat on your taxes, and it cannot be overemphasized that cheating or defrauding the government in any way is a dangerous practice. The following chapters will certainly not encourage any such action, either directly or by implication. However, if you want to really save some bucks legally (and who doesn't) then read on.

Chapter 2

Deductions

Deductions: who may take deductions—what may be deducted—how to use these deductions. A chart on the average deductions arranged by income; with an indication of the ages of the various contributors. Procedures of standard deductions. Medical deductions with step-by-step directions and examples of allowable deductions. Taxes that are allowable deductions; including the latest information on real estate, personal property, sale taxes and others. Interest deductions including methods of determining interest paid for a particular taxable year. Charitable contributions with examples. How to deduct losses due to casualty and theft. Miscellaneous allowable deductions and examples of their uses.

Taxpayers who itemize their personal deductions fall into three general categories: Those who claim anything and everything, as long as it seems believable; those who claim all that they are entitled to; and those who only claim those deductions for which they are absolutely sure.

The first category is the smallest, consisting perhaps of five percent of the total. These are frequently the disenchanted, disillusioned refugees of a previous generation; individuals whose faith in the fairness of government has been completely destroyed. They see their tax preparation as their only opportunity to "get even" with the lawmakers, and so they either fail to report their income, or they exaggerate their deductions.

When these taxpayers itemize their deductions on Schedule A of the Form 1040, there are some questions in their minds as to whether or not the Internal Revenue Service will accept their figures. The amounts of the deductions may appear too large or too small to the taxpayers, and they may or may not be able to substantiate the deductions.

The following chart, broken down into adjusted gross income groups, shows average adjusted gross incomes and various average deductions claimed for contributions, interest, taxes, and medical expenses. While this chart might be interesting for those who itemize deductions to compare their own deductions with these average amounts, it is certainly not to be considered that the Internal Revenue Service will necessarily allow these amounts. These figures are averages only, and should only be considered as such.

Income	Contributions	Interest	Taxes	Medical
$ 5,000-$ 6,000	301	760	594	808
6,000- 7,000	312	748	651	624
7,000- 8,000	291	767	673	622
8,000- 9,000	321	846	741	607
9,000- 10,000	314	899	809	557
10,000- 15,000	347	1090	1025	455
15,000- 20,000	421	1308	1400	412
20,000- 25,000	530	1538	1764	394
25,000- 30,000	663	1736	2169	391
30,000- 50,000	964	2221	2965	558

These average figures also tell us something of age groups for the respective income groups. As you can see, the average deductions for medical expenses becomes less and less as income increases. Probably, that is because young married people start their families, thereby incurring high medical expenses, at the time when their income is lowest. At the other end of the scale, these medical expenses increase again. This is most likely due to the high age of the people in this higher income group.

Also, please note that average contributions do not change much until the $15,000 income category, This simply indicates that until an individual is earning enough to provide the basic security and comfort that he needs, he is less inclined to be terribly concerned with the charitable needs of others.

Once again, these averages are in no way meant to imply that Internal Revenue Service will accept entries on your tax return just because they fall within these limits. The only point to be made here is that you should be prepared to substantiate your deductions with receipts, and if any deductions are greater than these averages, there is a good chance that they will cause an alarm to go off in the IRS computer and that you will be asked to provide evidence to support your deductions.

This is a standard procedure, and it is **not** an audit. Each Internal Revenue Service district is equipped with a computer to process the tax returns. As the return is received, the information is fed into the computer (without any regard to accuracy or fact). The computer then checks the accuracy, and evaluates the return. The computer is programmed to accept or reject various entries. When it comes to deduction entries, the computer has been programmed to accept all entries within certain limits. These limits are well guarded secrets, and may vary from one IRS district to the next.

If any of your entries exceed the limit, the entire return is kicked out for a human evaluation. This is the time that you might be asked to provide the receipts to prove your deductions. And the examiner who looks at your return might ask to see proof for deductions other than the one that the computer rejected.

MEDICAL DEDUCTIONS

The amount of medical expenses which may be deducted is the sum of the amount of medical expenses **paid** during the year (reduced by three percent of the adjusted gross income shown on line 15c of Form 1040), plus one-half of the payments made to a qualified accident and health insurance policy. The full amount of accident and health insurance is treated as a medical expense, but the rule allows the taxpayer to deduct one half (up to $150.00) without regard to the 3% reduction mentioned above. The remainder, whether it is 50% or more, can be listed as a medical expense, but it is subject to the 3% reduction rule.

Medicines and drugs qualify as medical expenses if they meet the following tests. They must be legally procured; they must be generally accepted as medicine and drugs. Such things as prescription drugs, aspirin, patent medicine, cough syrup, birth control pills, are commonly accepted to be deductible medicines and drugs. On the other side, such things as toothpaste, feminine hygiene products, deodorants, and cosmetics are not normally deductible. There has been some controversy over the status of flouride toothpaste, but the position of the Internal Revenue Service at this time is that such toothpaste is not a medicine or drug.

Medicines and drugs are subject to a reduction of their own. These deductible expenses must be reduced by one percent of the Adjusted Gross Income mentioned above before they can be added to the total medical expenses.

The list of qualified medical expenses is very long and very liberal. It includes legal abortion, ambulance service, crutches, sterilization, dental care, nursing, eye glasses or contact lenses, hospitalization, transportation, hearing aids, psychiatric care, X-Rays and medical laboratory work, and many others. Some of the seldom used, or frequently overlooked deductible expenses are contact lens insurance, air conditioning (when primarily for the purpose of alleviating an illness), mileage to and from medical service (at 7 cents per mile), meals (only when eaten inside a medical facility while being treated), and wigs advised by a doctor to avoid mental upset due to loss of hair.

John Smith has an Adjusted Gross Income of $12,000.00. His paid medical expenses during the year included: $426.00 for health insurance; $1,250.00 hospital bills; $890.00 doctor bills; $350.00 dentist bills; $120.00 for eyeglasses; $70.00 mileage (1,000 miles at 7 cents); and $400.00 for medicine and drugs. The first $150.00 of his health insurance is not subject to any reduction, but the remaining $270.00 must be added to the other medical expenses.

One percent of John's Adjusted Gross Income is $120.00, so his medicine and drug expense must first be reduced from $400.00 to $280.00. Then the $276.00 remaining insurance premium, and the other medical expenses may be added.

The total of all these expenses is $3,236.00. John's insurance paid $1,712.00 toward these expenses, leaving him with a net "out-of-pocket" expense $1,524.00. This is the amount that must be reduced by the three percent (of 12,000.00) factor ($360.00 in this case).

After deducting the $360.00, leaving a balance of $1,164.00, John should add in the $150.00 (the first portion of the health insurance). Therefore, John's total deductible medical expenses are $1,314.00. Since this is substantially more than the average for his wage bracket, he should also be prepared to provide proof of these expenses.

John should claim these expenses even though he might, for any reason, be unable to substantiate them. If he is certain, in good faith, that he incurred the expenses, they should be claimed. The worst thing that could happen is that the Internal Revenue Service might disallow all or part of the deduction.

DEDUCTIBLE TAXES

The Internal Revenue Service allows deductions for most state, local, federal, and foreign taxes paid. By allowing these deductions, the burden of double taxation is considerably eased.

As a general rule, the following tax categories are deductible: income tax; real estate tax; personal property tax; sales tax; gasoline tax; and other tax paid involving the production of income.

Not all money paid to the government is in the form of

taxes. Some examples of non-tax payments include: Postage; Driver's License Fee; Bridge or highway tolls; Auto Registration (part of this may be classified as a tax, but not all); Pension Fund payments; and Social Security contributions.

If you reside in a state that charges its own income tax, payments to that state for tax on your income is deductible on your federal tax return. That amount will be the total tax withheld from your pay, plus any other payments that you made during the year. If you received a refund during the year, the amount of the withholding must be reduced by the refund. If the refund exceeds the withholding, the refund must be declared as income.

Real estate taxes are deductible whether or not they are related to a trade or business, or related to the production of income. These taxes are always deducted in the year paid, and the deduction does **not** include any penalties or interest charged for delinquent payment of taxes.

All state and local gasoline taxes are deductible. The amount of this tax varies from state to state. The Internal Revenue Service provides a chart showing the rate for each state, along with the standard deduction amounts for different mileages driven. This chart provides the taxpayer with an acceptable deduction amount without the problem of saving gasoline receipts. In fact, unless you drive extensively in a motorhome, truck, or other vehicle with very low gasoline efficiency, the chart will actually give you a greater deduction than your actual expense.

Another chart that the Internal Revenue Service provides is for general sales tax. This chart, or group of charts, gives an amount of sales tax paid by income and family size. Again, these charts provide you with an easy amount, and since it is the amount that the government has recommended, you will not be questioned if you use them. However, in contrast with the gasoline tax chart, the sales tax chart is not necessarily a good deal for you.

As an example, the general sales tax from the State of California chart for a family of four with income of

$15,000.00 to $15,999.99 is only $227.00. This means taxable spending of $3,783.33. Since such a family would have disposable income of $11,000.00, more or less, they could very easily spend more than the $3,783.33 on taxable items.

Personal property tax is fully deductible and normally takes the form of a tax on personal belongings, autos, boats, trailers, mobilehomes, and furniture. By far the most common example of such a tax is the automobile registration tax, and only a portion of it is deductible. Every automobile, regardless of age or condition, pays a set fee (different from state to state) for registration. But, as additional amount is added to that set fee, and that additional amount is a tax on the value of the vehicle.

Some states provide that payments to unemployment or disability funds are deductible. The State of New Jersey, as an example, holds that contributions to state sickness and disability funds are deductible. On the other hand, New York and California laws, state that such expenses are not deductible.

Also, you may claim the amount of sales tax you pay on such major purchases as an automobile, mobilehome, furniture, and home improvements. This excess sales tax may be taken **in addition to** the general sales tax mentioned above. The reasoning behind this deduction being allowed is that normally such purchases are for large amounts, and as such are not paid for from the income of any one particular year. The money for the purchase was either saved over a period of years, or the purchase was made on a contract calling for payments to be spread over years in the future.

If you purchase a used car from a private party, you will not pay sales tax, as such. Instead, when you change the title of the vehicle into your own name, you will be assessed a "Use Tax," based either on the sales price or on the year, make, and model of the vehicle. This Use Tax may also be claimed as a deduction in the "Other Deductions" section of Schedule A, Form 1040.

INTEREST DEDUCTIONS

Nearly any type of interest paid or accrued during the year is deductible. Two notable exceptions are interest on a loan to buy insurance, and interest on a loan to buy tax-free municipal bonds or other securities. Also, there must be a valid debt before any interest deduction can be allowed.

The amount of interest payment which is deductible is not ordinarily subject to limitation, provided it was required by a valid debt or obligation and was actually paid **or accrued**. If an installment buyer pays carrying charges, it will be necessary to have the lender provide the deductible portion of those charges.

Earlier, it was mentioned that the interest on delinquent taxes was not deductible as tax. Such interest is, however, deductible as interest. The penalty for such delinquency is not deductible at all.

The most common types of loans are consumer loans, in which the interest is most commonly added to the amount of the loan proceeds before the first payment is made, regardless of the length of repayment. This type of interest is called, predictably, "Add On Interest." Normally, when you contact the bank or other lending institution for the amount of interest you paid in a given year, they will only tell you the total interest that was added to the loan, and leave it up to you to determine how much should apply to the year in question.

It should be pointed out that if your repayment schedule is spread over more than one year, you cannot take all of the interest as a deduction in a single year. You may elect either of two methods to calculate your deduction: First, the straight-line method, in which the interest is divided equally between the installments (that is, if there are twenty-four installments, you may apply 1/24 of the interest to each of the installments made in the tax year). Second, you may use the Sum-of-the-Digits method (also known as the Rule of 78's), which is much more complicated, but will be a more accurate reflection of the true interest expense.

The Sum-of-the-Digits is time consuming, but will permit you to deduct your interest expense at an accelerated rate. You must work with fractions in computing this method, and it will be helpful if you have an adding machine and/or a pocket calculator handy.

To figure your interest deduction with this method, you first add up all of the payments (not the amounts of the payments, but the payments themselves). As an example, if you have a twenty-four payment schedule, you would add 24 + 23 + 22 + 21 + 20 + 19 + 18, and so forth down to 1. In this example, the sum of the digits is 300, but for different length repayment schedules, the sum would naturally be different.

Next, you must calculate the number of payments made with the year. If this loan was made in April, for instance, with the first payment made in May, then you would have made eight payments during the year. You always count down with this method, so you assign the numbers 24, 23, 22, 21, 20, 19, 18, and 17 to the payments you made. Then you add up these numbers. The total should be 164.

Finally you make a fraction of the two sums: 164/300. This fraction is the portion of the total interest that can be applied to the current year's deductions. As you can see, more than half of the interest can be deducted, even though only one-third of the payments have been made. Incidently, the name "Rule of 78's comes from the fact that the sum of digits 1 through 12 equals 78.

An easier way to do this calculation is to make friends with a bank loan officer and have him do it for you. All he will do is either look it up in a book of already prepared charts, or have a computer do it.

One word of caution should be noted. Under no circumstances should you deduct more than the total interest charged. If you elect the Sum-of-the-Digits method, it could be very easy to miscalculate, since the deductible amount will change from one year to the next.

An example of such a loan could be as follows: Harry Howe borrowed $1,000.00 from his friendly, hometown bank, and agreed to repay the loan at 10% interest per year, to be added on to the loan proceeds. The total interest charged was $200.00, and Harry's terms called for 24 equal monthly installments to begin on May 15. In the first year, Harry is eligible to claim an interest deduction for the first eight installments.

With the straight-line method, he would claim 8/24 of the total interest charged, or $66.66. With the Sum-of-the-Digits method, he would claim 164/300 of the total interest charged, or $109.33. In the second year, the straight-line deduction would be 12/24 (he made payments in each month of the year), or $100.00.

The second-year, Sum-of-the-Digits deductions would be calculated by taking the sum of the next twelve consecutive digits in the countdown mentioned above (16 + 15 + 14 + 13, etc).   That fraction would come to 126/300, and the deduction for the second year would be $84.00.

The third year deduction could not exceed the remaining, unclaimed interest (only four installments remain). With the straight-line method, $166.66 has already been deducted, so the balance remaining is $33.34. With the accelerated, Sum-of-the-Digits method, the prior deductions total $193.33, leaving a balance of only $6.67.

This loophole permits you to control your deductible expenses so that you might be able to have greater deductions at a time when your income is greater, thereby saving in your taxes.

Other interest deductions that are frequently overlooked are loan fees, points, and pre-payment penalties. Many lending institutions make such charges, and these charges are often missed when determining the deductible interest.

Loan fees, unless they are definitely labelled for such services as appraisal or commitment, are deductible. Points are normally charged on real estate loans. They consist of a percentage of the loan amount, and are charged as a sort of "bonus" interest, and are paid at the time the loan is paid. Such points are always deductible as interest, but are not always listed on the statement of interest paid which you receive from the bank.

Many lenders also have a condition for a prepayment penalty written into the loan agreement. This penalty is assessed if the loan is paid off, or even substantially reduced, within the first five years of the loan terms. Such a pre-payment penalty is deductible as interest in the year it is paid.

CHARITABLE CONTRIBUTIONS

Contributions to qualified organizations are deductible by individuals who itemize their deductions. In order for an organization to qualify it must be organized and operated exclusively for charitable, religious, educational, scientific, or literary purposes. Also qualifying are organizations dedicated to the prevention of cruelty to children or animals.

Contributions do not need to be cash. Many people donate used clothing and other personal belongings to such groups as the Salvation Army. Such donations are deductible, but, if the items are used, you must determine the useful value of them. A used coat cannot be deductible at its cost, even though it might be in excellent condition.

Contributions to public or private libraries are normally deductible. For instance, an attorney might donate law books to the library of his local bar association. Such a gift is normally deductible. Any individual might contribute old books to a public library, and deduct the value of those books as a charitable contribution on his Schedule A.

There are many such examples of "other than cash" donations. The primary thing that you must remember is that the organization that receives the gift must meet the requirements of qualification listed above. A donation, contribution, or gift, whether it is in cash or other form, given to your favorite nephew is not deductible, even if said nephew is the most deserving charity case you know.

Whenever possible, you should get receipts for your contributions. Those agencies which accept non-cash donations are very willing to give a written receipt, showing the value of the gift, and the date. They are most cooperative in assisting you in determining the value of your gift.

But even if you do not get a receipt, you are entitled to claim your donation as a deduction. The Internal Revenue Service understands that we are faced almost daily with requests from deserving charities and other groups. Such organizations as the March of Dimes and the Heart Fund frequently have displays asking for loose change to be donated. There is never a provision for a receipt at one of these displays, so it is accepted that a family could contribute up to $100.00 per year without getting a receipt.

LOSSES—CASUALTY AND THEFT

Any loss of personal property, due to fire, theft, accident, or any other casualty is deductible. Such a deduction is subject to certain limitations. First, the loss must be adjusted by the amount of insurance coverage, if any. Second, the remaining loss must be reduced by $100.00 for each incident.

If your automobile was completely destroyed by an accident, you may be eligible to claim a casualty loss deduction. As an example, if your automobile had a replacement cost of $2,000.00, and your insurance paid only what they considered to be the market value of $1,850.00, from which they took their $200.00 deductible (not to be confused with tax deductibility). You would only receive $1,650.00. The $350.00 excess loss could be claimed as a casualty loss, subject to the $100.00 reduction, leaving you with a deduction of $250.00.

A casualty loss is generally one that happens suddenly. In other words, if your automobile becomes damaged due to rust or some other gradual effect, you may not claim the casualty loss as a deduction. If your home is damaged by termites, you can not claim the loss, but if it is destroyed by a hurricane, you can.

If you have more than one incident of casualty loss in a given year, you must complete Form 4684, which calls for you to explain the nature of the property, the value, and also the type of accident that caused the loss. This must be done separately for each loss. The Form 4684 provides enough space for three such losses.

MISCELLANEOUS DEDUCTIONS

This section is a catch-all for deductible expenses that do not fit any other category. Such expenses include, alimony, child care, legal fees, education, employee business expense, subscriptions and dues, recordkeeping expenses, tax preparation expense, accounting expense, employment agency fees, union dues, uniforms, protective clothing, tools of trade, and investment counseling fees.

Alimony is deductible, but child support is not. On the other hand, child support is not taxable to the person receiving it, but alimony received is fully taxable income.

The itemized deduction for household and dependent care expenses has been replaced with a nonrefundable income tax credit. This new approach to what was formerly an itemized deduction contains the following features: A maximum credit of $400.00 for one and $800.00 for two or more qualifying dependents which replaces the former maximum deduction of $400.00 per month or $4,800.00 per year for child or dependent care expenses; The credit is not reduced by the taxpayer's excess income as the old deduction; Child care expenses incurred outside the home count the same as those in the home; Payments to relatives can qualify; The qualifications for eligibility have been liberalized.

The Tax Reform Act of 1976 replaces the deduction with a credit against the amount of tax due. All of the prior rules for determining for whom the credit may be claimed still exist, but the door is opened to many individuals who could not benefit in the past. Since it is no longer included as an itemized deduction, people who choose the standard deduction can now gain from this change.

The credit is twenty percent of the child care expenses during the year up to a maximum of $2,000.00 in expenses for one child, or up to $4,000.00 if there are two or more. This change will benefit many people, but it will cost some others (those in higher tax brackets).

In addition to dependent children under age 15, the following individuals qualify for this credit: A dependent who is physically or mentally incapable of caring for himself, regardless of age; The spouse of the taxpayer if he or she is physically or mentally incapable of caring for himself, regardless of age.

Legal fees are only deductible if they were incurred in income production. If you hire an attorney to draw up a will, such fees are not deductible. However, if you retain an attorney to assist you in the collection of a bad debt, his fees may be claimed as a deduction. Similarly, if you retain an attorney to assist you with the management of your funds, or to assist you with tax problems, those expenses are deductible.

Education expenses are deductible in some cases. If your employer required you to take courses to improve your job performance you may deduct the expenses, including mileage, of such education. However, if you are taking courses specifically designed to prepare you for another job, you may not deduct them. On that note, the expenses of a student while attending school prior to entering the job market are not deductible, either to the student, or to the parents if that student is their dependent.

If you work on more than one job, or if your employer requires that you travel from one job site to another at your own expense, the expense of the travel between these locations is deductible. This is not to be confused with the expense of commuting from your home to the job. Commuting is not deductible. Along these lines, though, you can deduct any expense that you incur for the benefit of your employer.

Union dues are totally deductible. Dues paid to professional or trade organizations are also deductible. Also, if you subscribe to any publication that will assist you to perform your job in a better manner, such subscription is deductible.

Since the Internal Revenue Service requires that you keep accurate records and receipts of your income and expenses, you may also deduct the expenses of such recordkeeping. Such things as a Safe Deposit Box and a home filing cabinet are well established as deductible expenses. The service charge for your checking account is another such expense, but is has not yet been accepted by IRS. Inasmuch as the IRS auditors accept cancelled checks as proof of deductible payments, it is only a matter of time until the checking account service charge will be recognized as a deductible expense.

Any assistance you get in the preparation of your tax return is deductible, whether you hire a tax practitioner, or simply buy this book or one of the many books on the market that show you how to fill out the forms.

If you use the services of an employment agency to find employment in your trade, such fees as they might charge are deductible expenses. However, if you use such an agency to find a job for the first time, or to change your type of employment, you may not claim the deduction.

Uniforms, such as a nurse or a waitress might be required to wear, are deductible expense. This deduction includes the purchase of the uniforms, as well as the cleaning and maintenance. Special shoes designed for individuals that are on their feet all the time are deductible, as are support hosiery for those individuals. If you should choose to clean your uniforms at home, rather than having them professionally cleaned, you can still claim the cost of such cleaning by keeping track of the actual expense of soap, water, etc.

Many individuals are required to wear safety shoes and other protective clothing. All such items are deductible. Also, an individual can claim the cost of the tools of his trade as a deductible expense. If such tools have a life expectancy of one year or less, the entire cost of the tools is deductible in the year of purchase. In the case of tools that last longer, the cost must be spread over the reasonable life of the tools, and the deduction for that cost must be taken in proportion to the life.

Finally, any expense that you incur in the production of income is deductible. An example of such an expense might be an investment counselor, retained to aid you make your investment decisions.

Chapter 3

Tax Free
Fringe Benefits

Tax-free fringe benefits: the key to building your wealth. How the employer and employee benefit from a profit-sharing plan. What profit-sharing is and how it benefits you. Income averaging and long-term capital gains: a further advantage. A typical example of profit-sharing. Using medical expenses and health plans to your advantage. Tax exempt life insurance. Mileage expense deductions. A vacation expense that is tax deductible and how to arrange it.

Despite the changes which the 1976 laws made in the method of taxing capital gains and payouts to employees, profit-sharing plans still remain the tax law's biggest and best wealth builder. Why? Simply because the special treatment the law grants cannot be matched by any other plan. In general, this special treatment allows the employer to deduct his contributions. Also, the plan is held and invested by a profit-sharing trust, which is exempt from all Federal income tax. Finally, the participating employee does not pay any tax on either the contributions, OR the income (interest, etc) that is gained from the investment of the contributions, until he draws it.

Make no mistake! The government will insist that the tax must be paid eventually. However, the advantages are:

1. You will ordinarily draw this profit-sharing money at your retirement. At the present time, you are probably in your peak earning years. Subsequently, you are most likely in the highest tax bracket you will reach. However, upon retirement, your income will almost certainly be much lower than it is now. That means that when you receive the proceeds from your profit-sharing plan, you will be in a lower tax bracket.

2. A significant portion of your profit-sharing money will qualify for long-term capital gains treatment. Enter the long-term capital gains portion on Schedule D. This amount is reduced by 50% before it is added to your taxable income.

3. The rest of the profit-sharing windfall is taxed as ordinary income. However, that remaining portion qualifies for a special 10-year Averaging break. You will need to complete form 4792 to get this advantage.

Also, you might benefit from income averaging to further reduce the amount of tax you owe on profit-sharing income.

Now, if you are self-employed in a small business, you can set up a profit-sharing plan for yourself. In order to do this, you must be the only employee, and you must provide for covering additional employees if and when they are hired.

The net result of profit-sharing is that the employer gets a deduction for his contribution, and the employee does not need to pay income tax on either the contribution or the dividends of the plan until he draws it. Also, when he finally must pay taxes on the money, chances are that he will have to pay less than he would had he received the money while working.

Following is a typical illustration:

Fred Jones is a loyal employee of the ABC Corporation, a small, closely-held company. He has been with the company for 20 years and has received an average salary of $15,000 per year during that time. Over the years, the company has contributed $18,000 to a profit-sharing trust for Fred, and the trust company has judiciously invested the money. Fred is now ready for retirement, and his profit-sharing plan is worth $40,000.

The actual cost to ABC Corporation for the contributions to Fred's profit-sharing plan was $8,640 after taxes. If they had given him salary or bonus of $18,000, the cost to the company would have been $19,782 (or $9,495 after taxes). This difference in dollars is due to the 50% reduction in taxes available on long term capital gains.

If Fred had received the $18,000 in salary, he would have paid tax of $3,960 on it, leaving him with a net of $14,040. And had he invested the money, his income from the investment would have been taxable. Assuming he did as well as the trust company, he would have received $17,160 in investment income ($13,385 after taxes) over the years.

Of the $40,000 Fred receives at retirement, $22,000 will qualify for long-term capital gains.

	Actual	Taxable
Long Term Capital Gains	$22,000.00	$11,000.00
Ordinary Income	18,000.00	18,000.00
TOTAL	$40,000.00	$29,000.00
Tax on Capital Gains	$1,309	
Tax on Ordinary Income (Form 4792)	3,168	
TOTAL TAX LIABILITY	$4,477	
Net from profit-sharing method		$35,523.00
Net from salary method		27,425.00
DIFFERENCE		$ 8,098.00

So, as you can see, Fred comes off $8,098 better through profit-sharing. And, it has actually cost ABC Corporation $1,782 less to accomplish this.

If you are an employee who is not covered by a profit-sharing plan at the present time, you should persuade your employer to look into the possibilities. If you are an employer, you should immediately speak to your tax consultant and have him set up a profit-sharing plan that fits your needs.

If your employer does not have a profit-sharing plan and is not receptive to your suggestion, you are not out in the cold completely. You can obtain an Individual Retirement Act Account through most banks, savings and loan associations, and insurance companies.

The Keogh Plan is provided for by law to give retirement income to small businessmen. Most banks and saving institutions have trust departments set up to handle these.

You may deposit 15% of your gross income into this account, up to a maximum of $1,500 annually, and deduct the amount of your deposit from your taxable income. If you are self-employed, this deposit and deduction may be as high as $7,500 per year, through a Keogh Plan, which may be set up at any of the institutions mentioned above.

There is a drawback! If you draw your money out of any such plan, whether through your employer or on your own, you must pay tax on all of the money in the year drawn. There is one exception to this stringent rule: If you re-invest the entire amount into another IRA account in the same year, it is considered a "roll-over," and is not taxable.

MEDICAL BENEFITS

The income (or reimbursement) received by an employee from his employer to cover medical expenses for himself, his spouse and his dependents is not considered taxable. This includes health insurance, but it does not stop there. The tax law states that employer contributions to health plans to compensate employees for

Form **2106**
Department of the Treasury
Internal Revenue Service

Employee Business Expenses

▶ Attach to Form 1040.

1976

Your name
SYLVESTER SAVAGE

Social security number
456:78:9012

Occupation in which expenses were incurred
SALESMAN

Employer's name
ACME WIDGET Co.

Employer's address
ST. LOUIS, MO.

Instructions

Include all expenses you paid or incurred as an employee, or expenses you charged to your employer (for example, through use of credit cards), or expenses for which you received an advance, allowance, or reimbursement. For a more detailed explanation of these expenses, see instructions for Form 1040.

Include business expenses for which you were paid (reimbursed)

by your employer in Part I, line 6, unless they are included on your Form W–2. Report any such amounts shown on your Form W–2 as wages on Form 1040, line 9. Check with your employer if you doubt whether the payment is included on your Form W–2. For a detailed explanation of the rules for deductions for travel, entertainment, and gift expenses, see **Publication 463**, Travel, Entertainment, and Gift Expenses.

Use Form 3903 to compute any moving expense deduction.

PART I.—Employee Business Expenses Deductible in Computing Adjusted Gross Income on Form 1040, Line 15c

1 Travel expenses while away from home on business (number of days) **150**		
(a) Airplane, boat, railroad, etc., fares		
(b) Meals and lodging	$3,900 -	
(c) Automobile expenses (from Part IV)	4,461 -	
(d) Other (specify) ▶		
Total travel expenses		8,361 -
2 Transportation expenses (not between home and work and not incurred while away from home overnight):		
(a) Airplane, bus, railroad, taxi, etc., fares		
(b) Automobile expenses (from Part IV)		
(c) Other (specify) ▶		
Total transportation expenses		

28

3 Outside salesperson's expenses:

    (a) Automobile expenses (from Part IV) . . . . ▲

    (b) Other (specify) ▲

        Total outside salesperson's expenses . . . .

4 Employee expenses other than traveling, transportation, and outside salesperson's expenses to the extent of reimbursement . . | 8,361 |

5   Total of lines 1, 2, 3, and 4 . . . . | 8,400 |

6 Less: Employer's payments for above expenses (other than amounts included on Form W–2) . . . .

7 Excess expenses (line 5 less line 6). Enter here and include on Form 1040, line 39 . . . . | 39 |

8 Excess payments (line 6 less line 5). Enter here and include on Form 1040, line 36 . . . .

PART II.—Employee Business Expenses which are Deductible if You Itemize Deductions on Schedule A (Form 1040)

1 Business expenses other than those included above (specify) ▲

2   Total . . . .

If you itemize your deductions instead of using the standard deduction, deduct under Miscellaneous Deductions, Schedule A (Form 1040).

PART III.—Additional Information to be Furnished When Claiming a Deduction for Educational Expenses

1 Name of educational institution or activity ▲

2 Address ▲

3 Were you required to undertake this education to meet the minimum educational requirements to qualify in your employment, trade or business? . . . . ☐ Yes ☐ No

4 Will the study program undertaken qualify you for a new trade or business? . . . . ☐ Yes ☐ No

5 If your answer to question 3 or 4 is No, state the reason for obtaining the additional education and show the relationship between the courses taken and your employment during the period ▲

6 List the principal subjects studied at the educational institution or describe your educational activity ▲

PART IV.—Automobile Expenses (Use either the regular or the optional method.)

	Automobile 1	Automobile 2	Automobile 3
A. Months automobile held for business use	12 months	___ months	___ months
B. Total mileage for months in A	30,000 miles	___ miles	___ miles
C. Portion of total mileage applicable to business	30,000 miles	___ miles	___ miles

Regular Method: (Include expenses only for the number of months indicated in A above.)

	Automobile 1	Automobile 2	Automobile 3
1 Gasoline, oil, lubrication, etc.	$ 1,300 —		
2 Repairs	200 —		
3 Tires, supplies, etc.	300 —		
4 Other: (a) Insurance	200 —		
(b) Taxes			
(c) Tags and licenses	104 —		
(d) Interest	450 —		
(e) Miscellaneous			
5 Total	$ 2,554 —		
6 Percentage of expense applicable to business (line C above divided by line B above)	100 %	%	%
7 Business portion (line 5 multiplied by line 6)	$ 2,554 —		
8 Depreciation from Part VI, column (h)	1,667 —		
9 Line 8 divided by 12 months	139 -		
10 Multiply line 9 by A, above	1,667 -		
11 Total (line 7 plus line 10) (see line 17)	4,221 -		

Optional Method: (The standard mileage rate applies to the total business miles (line C, above) of all automobiles that have not been or are not considered fully depreciated under the straight-line method. For automobiles that have been or are considered fully depreciated under the straight-line method, the standard mileage rate is 10 cents per mile for all business mileage.)

The optional method cannot be used if you have claimed depreciation in a prior year using a method other than straight line (or if you have claimed additional first-year depreciation). Use of the optional

12 Enter 15,000 miles or the mileage on line C above, whichever is smaller		_____ miles
13 Multiply line 12 by 15¢ and enter result		

30

14 Any excess of line C over 15,000 miles . . . . _____ miles | method will not affect a deduction for interest relating to the automobile nor deductions for State and local taxes (other than those included in the cost of gasoline).

15 Multiply line 14 by 10¢ and enter result . . . . .
16 Total (line 13 plus line 15) . . . . . .

Summary:

17 Enter the amount from line 11 or line 16, whichever is used . | 4,221 —
18 Add parking fees and tolls. . . . . | 240 —
19 Total. Enter here and in appropriate sections of Part I, page 1. | 4,461 —

PART V.—Computation of Automobile Basis

Old Car Traded In:

1 (a) Total mileage accumulated . . . . _____ miles
  (b) Portion applicable to business . . _____ miles
  (c) Percentage applicable to business
    (line (b) divided by line (a)) . . . _____ %
2 Purchase price or other basis . . . .
3 Less: Trade-in allowance . . . . .
4 Difference (line 2 less line 3) . . . .
5 Line 4 multiplied by percentage on line
  1(c). . . . .
6 Less gain or plus (loss) on previous
  trade-in. . . . .
7 Difference (line 5 less line 6) . . . .
8 Depreciation allowed or allowable . .
9 Gain (line 8 less line 7) or loss (line 7
  less line 8) on business portion of car .

Present Car:

10 Purchase price or other basis . . . . | $6,000 —
11 Less: Estimated salvage value . . . | 1,000 —
12 Balance (line 10 less line 11) . . . | 5,000 —
13 Line 12 multiplied by percentage on line
  6 of Part IV . . . . | 5,000 —
14 Less gain or plus (loss) on line 9 . . | —0—
15 Basis for computing depreciation . . | 5,000 —

Note: If you acquired the vehicle for cash only, or by trade-in of another vehicle not used in business, complete only lines 10 through 15. If acquired by trade-in of another vehicle previously used in business, complete lines 1 through 15. (Recompute the basis for depreciation each succeeding year if the percentage of business use changes.)

PART VI.—Depreciation of Automobile

Make and style of vehicle (a)	Date acquired (b)	Basis (From line 15, Part V) (c)	Age when acquired (d)	Depreciation allowed in prior years (e)	Method of computing depreciation (f)	Rate (%) or life (years) (g)	Depreciation for a year (h)
1976 Toyota	JAN 76	5,000 —	NEW	—0—	SL	3	

injury or sickness are not taxable to the employee, but are a deductible expense of the employer. A health plan as defined "may cover one or more employees, and there may be different plans for different employees. An accident or health plan may be insured or non-insured, and it is not necessary that the plan be in writing."

Let's look at an example. Suppose your income is in the $15,000 per year range, a 22% tax bracket, and you have $1,000 in doctor and dentist bills for the year. Your deduction must first be reduced by 3% of your income. That amounts to $450, leaving you with $550 in deductions. The tax effect on that amounts to only $121 in saving for you ($550 x 22%). On the other hand, if your employer pays for that medical expense, he can deduct the entire $1,000 as a business expense.

In the first example, you are out $879 ($1,000 minus $121). If the employer pays, he will be out of pocket only $600-$700, depending on his tax bracket.

An attractive side benefit of a plan like this is that you do not have to get sick to take advantage of it. It covers annual physical checkups, as well as illness and injury.

LIFE INSURANCE

One of the most popular forms of tax-exempt compensation is employer-paid group life insurance. Its popularity is understandable—the premiums are deductible by the employer; and the first $50,000 of coverage paid by the employer is tax free to the employee.

AUTOMOBILE EXPENSE

Suppose you are a salesman, and you travel 30,000 miles per year in your own car. Let's also assume you are an underpaid salesman and you want a salary increase. If your employer grants you a raise of $1,200 per year, it will cost him a total of $1,320 per year with his additional payroll taxes, and you are going to take home only $936 more in your paycheck. But, if he increases your mileage allowance by 4 cents per mile, his cost will be only $1,200, and you will still receive the $936 after taxes. This mileage allowance is also deductible by the employer.

This type of mileage deduction is allowed to the self-employed individual provided his mileage is a legitimate business expense.

VACATION TIME

Internal Revenue Service often takes a very dim view on employer-paid vacations. However, if you go about it properly, you can benefit from this loophole. Follow these steps:

1. Once you have planned your vacation, arrange with your employer to travel on business to a location near your vacation site.

2. Be sure that you actually conduct the business involved. If you fail to do this, IRS will certainly disallow all of your expenses.

3. Keep complete records of your expenses, so that you can accurately separate business from personal expenses.

Those expenses that are deductible will be transportation between your place of employment and the location of the outside business, plus your meals and lodging while actually on business. The expenses of your spouse and family are not deductible, ordinarily.

Chapter 4

Dividends

Dividends: what they are and what they mean to the average wage earner. A word about "double" taxation. Dividend exclusion allowance for you and your spouse. A way that your kids can actually save you money through stock and dividend dispersal. A chart showing a typical dividend dispersal plan, and its use in setting up one of your own. The rules and drawbacks concerning this type of plan. Other ways to minimize your taxes through companies paying distribution of reserves. Municipal and arbetrage bonds: their possibilities and uses.

For income tax purposes, the term "dividend" means any distribution made by a corporation to its stockholders out of its earnings and profits. Any dividend that fits this description is taxable to the person receiving it. This represents a **double** taxation, since the corporation has already paid income tax on its income, and the dividends are normally paid from the "after-taxes" profit of the corporation.

You can scream and complain until you are blue in the face about the unfairness of this double tax, but you will end up paying anyway. That is the law, and short of convincing Congress to make a radical change, there is nothing you can do about it. So, the secret is to manage your stock holdings in such a way as to minimize the tax effect on the dividends you receive. There are several ways to accomplish this.

Every individual is entitled to a "dividend exclusion" of $100.00. What this means is that each person is permitted to reduce the total of his dividends by $100.00 before adding it to his income. A husband and wife filing jointly have an exclusion of $200.00.

Obviously, one way to avoid tax on your dividends is to make sure that your holdings will not pay in excess of $100.00 per person. You can do this by limiting the amount of money you invest in stocks, or by investing in companies that do not ordinarily pay dividends. Such companies normally plow profits back into growth and expansion, and at least in theory, your stock becomes worth more.

If you have children, you can have stocks issued in the names of those children. The dividends would be taxable to the children, but each child could earn up to $2,450.00 without owing any tax. You would have to own quite a lot of stock to receive dividends in that amount.

Let's look at an imaginary family of four. The father is a reasonably successful businessman, with an annual income of $16,000.00. The mother does not work outside the home. The eldest daughter is 20 years old, and a junior in college. The youngest daughter is 17 years old, and will graduate from high school next year. This family has accumulated a modest fortune of $25,000.00 over the years. At the present time, the bulk of the money is in long term certificates of deposit at their bank, earning 6½% interest.

If this money was invested in the stock market, in carefully selected, solid companies, the resulting increase in income would be close to $500.00 per year. And much of that income, if not all of it, could be distributed in such a way that no taxes would be paid. Here is how it works:

50 shares of XYZ Corporation at $23.00 in the name of either father or mother	$1,150.00
500 shares of XYZ Corporation at $23.00, in the name of the oldest daughter	$11,500.00
500 shares of XYZ Corporation at $23.00 in the name of youngest daughter	$11,500.00
1050 shares total	$24,150.00

XYZ Corporation is a solid company with a proven record of success. XYZ Corporation pays annual dividends of $2.00 per share, and has not missed a dividend payment in 50 years.

The resulting dividends from those stocks, would be as follows:

50 shares of parents	$100.00
500 shares of oldest daughter	$1,000.00
500 shares of youngest daughter	$1,000.00
Total dividend income	$2,100.00

The bank was paying 6½% interest, or a total of $1,625.00 annually. The increase in actual income is $475.00 per year.

The father, you will recall, was in the $16,000.00 salary range. That puts him in an income tax bracket of 28%. If the stocks were all in his name, the tax on the dividend income would be $588.00, reducing the net income to $1,512.00.

However, by distributing the shares as shown above, the family has avoided the payment of any tax on the dividends, as follows:

100 shares of parents (subject to $200.00 exclusion) produced $200.00 income—NOT TAXABLE
1000 shares of oldest daughter (subject to $100.00 exclusion) produced $1,000.00 income, reduced to $900.00 by the exclusion. This is less than the $2,350.00 she is permitted to earn without tax, so even though the dividends were taxable, she has no tax liability—NO TAX DUE
1000 shares of youngest daughter—same as for oldest—NO TAX DUE

It should be pointed out that there are some drawbacks to this plan. The most obvious is that the shares are not under the direct control of the father, so he must have trust in his daughters' judgement.

In order to qualify these ''gifts'' as a tax-saving method, certain elements are required. Gifts of property to members of a family, frequently motivated by a desire to spread the income and thereby reduce the donor's taxes are carefully examined by the Internal Revenue Service in every instance. These gifts can be up to $3000. per year not taxable to the recipient nor deductible by the donor. The essential requirements of such a gift are:

1. The donor must be competent to make the gift. That is, he must be capable of making decisions concerning his property.

2. The person receiving the gift must be capable of handling his or her own affairs.

3. There must be a clear and unmistakable intention on the part of the donor to divest himself of title and control of the gift. The transfer must be immediate, absolute, and irrevocable.

4. The irrevocable transfer of the legal title and control of the entire gift to the recipient, so that the donor cannot exercise any further act of control over it.

5. There must be a delivery by the donor to the recipient of the gift.

6. And, finally, the gift must be accepted by the recipient.

The last drawback to this plan is that the parents might lose the right to claim the daughters as dependents. If the $1,000.00 they each receive is more than one-half of their support, the parents may not claim them. With the daughter in college, there is little doubt that her support might be questionable.

Another way to minimize your taxes on dividends is to choose companies that pay distributions from reserves. As mentioned above, only those dividends coming from earnings and profits are taxable. I should not mention any names of such stocks, but any reputable stock broker can advise you of these opportunities.

Municipal bonds are another investment possibility that offers tax free income. Interest received from obligations of a state, territory, or other political subdivision, such as a city, county, township, or district, is not taxable. In fact, such interest does not need to be reported as income at all.

There are a few restrictions involving such bonds. First, interest on "arbetrage bonds," is taxable. An arbetrage bond is one where a major part of the proceeds will be used to invest in other, higher yield, securities or obligations. Also, bonds issued by a nonprofit corporation for the purpose of stimulating industrial development within a political subdivision are subject to income tax. Finally, the bond must specifically agree to pay interest. An open account indebtedness of a city, county, or other political subdivision does not qualify for tax free status.

Chapter 5

Capital Gains

Capital gains: how the government decides on and defines what is, or is not, a capital gain. Exceptions to the capital gains qualifications. Capital gains tax rate for 1976 and beyond: the Tax Reform Act of 1976 will change the time limit on this type of income. How this Act applies to losses, and how future losses will be taxed. Examples of offsetting capital gains with capital losses, and how to accomplish these transactions. Capital gains and the family residence: how to compute and adjust the actual profit made in selling a residence. An example of such a sale. Exemptions for senior citizens on residence sales.

First, we should define the term "Capital Gain." Capital Gain (or Loss) is any gain or loss from the sale or exchange of a capital asset. And a capital asset is property other than;

1. Property held **primarily** for sale to customers in the ordinary course of trade or business, including inventory assets. I emphasize the word primarily because the Supreme Court of the United States has defined that word as meaning "of first importance." In other words, even though you might purchase shares of stock with the thought in mind that you will sell it if you can make a

profit, such intent on your part is only **substantial**, not **primary**. And the gain (or loss) is subject to Capital Gains;

2. Depreciable property used in business;

3. Real property used in the trade or business, such as the land upon which the business is located;

4. Short-term, non-interest bearing Government obligations (either State or Federal) issued on a discount basis. Short term means not over one year.

5. A copyright or similar property held by the person who created it.

6. Accounts or notes receivable acquired in the ordinary course of trade or business.

What all this boils down to is that most types of "non-business" property, such as stocks, bonds, residences, personal automobiles, household furnishings, jewelry, boats, airplanes, etc. owned and used for personal or investment purposes are capital assets. The advantage of Capital Gains over ordinary income, is that these gains are taxed at only one-half the ordinary rate, if the property is held for a certain period of time.

The Tax Reform Act of 1976 has set new time limits for Capital Gains as follows:

For assets to qualify for long-term Capital Gains treatment, you will have to hold them for more than nine months in 1977 and more than twelve months thereafter. For sales in 1976, or prior, the holding period is six months.

If you must sell an asset at a loss, it is better to take a short term capital loss, which can be subtracted dollar for dollar from your ordinary income, subject to limitations. The limitations have also been changed by the 1976 Tax Reform Act as follows: In 1976, you can claim capital losses only up to $1,000.00 against your ordinary income. If your losses are greater than $1,000.00, the excess must be carried forward to subsequent years. However, in 1977, the maximum amount that you can claim against your ordinary income goes to $2,000.00, and to $3,000.00 thereafter.

Let's say that you have purchased a vacant lot as an investment. The purchase price of the lot was $2,500.00 in

1972. After you bought the lot, the city required that you pay the costs of installing curbs, gutters, and sidewalks. That cost you another $1,200.00. In 1976, you sell the lot for $7,000.00. Your net gain on the transaction is $3,300.00, but you only have to pay tax on one-half of that gain, or $1,650.00.

Let's further assume that you own 200 shares of a stock that you purchased in 1971 at a price of $40.00 per share. Your investment in that stock is $8,000.00, but in the years since you plunged, the value or price of the stock has dropped to $25.00 per share, and has been holding steady near that price for some time now.

You know that the profit from that vacant lot will result in some tax for you, so you decide to sell the stock to offset that gain. You receive $5,000.00 for the stock, which is a long-term loss of $3,000.00. That loss is offset directly against the gain of $3,300.00 from the vacant lot. Your net long-term gain is now only $300.00, and you will have to pay tax on only $150.00.

Now you have $3,300.00 + $5,000.00 in cash in your pocket. You can repurchase the 200 shares of stock and have your $3,300.00 virtually tax free. Remember, the price of the stock had been stable recently, so the chances are pretty good that you will have to pay pretty much the same price as you received in the sale. The thing to remember is that you **must** wait at least 30 days from the date of the sale before you repurchase. If you do not wait the required length of time, the transaction will be ruled a "wash sale," and your loss will be disallowed. The total cost to you will be a couple of brokers' fees for the sale and purchase of the stock (about $100.00), and the tax savings to you will be in the $400.00—$600.00 neighborhood, depending on your income bracket.

It is prudent to mention at this point that there are some bad aspects of long-term capital gains. The foremost of these is in the sale of a personal residence.

If a family purchased a residence in 1946, at a cost of $9,500.00, and lived in it for thirty years, it is safe to assume that they will be able to sell it at a substantial profit.

The purchase price, plus whatever permanent improvements they have added during their ownership, is the basis for computing the profit. If the sale price in 1976 is $37,500.00, then the difference between the sale price and the basis is long-term capital gains, after adjusting for any costs of sale, such as commissions, etc.

In this example, the purchase price was $9,500.00, and we can assume an additional $4,000.00 for an extra bedroom and bathroom that was added in 1952. The real estate salesman earned a commission of $1,875.00 for selling the house, and other costs involved in the sale amounted to $400.00. The basis after all these adjustments is $15,775.00. The sale price was $37,500.00, and so the net capital gains (long-term) from this sale is $21,725.00. It should be noted that any real improvements and additions that remain with the house are deductible in this way.

Now $32,000.00 cash is no small amount, but if they wanted to buy a comparable house, they would end up $5,500.00 in debt, with a house no better than the one they sold.

Now that might sound pretty good to you, but consider this. Income tax must be paid on one-half of that profit. Such a tax could amount to $2,500.00—$4,000.00, depending on your tax bracket. This reduces your profit by that same amount, so right away the sugar pill starts to take on a bitter taste.

Now, if you really want to ruin your appetite, read on. Our family can put off the payments of this tax by purchasing a different residence within eighteen months of the date of sale. Please note, they do not **avoid** the tax, they merely put off paying the tax on the profit at this time. That profit will be added to any profit they might realize if and when they sell the new home.

Suppose they do not choose to purchase a new home. Okay, they report the long-term capital gain on their tax return for this year. Sounds reasonable, you say? You say since they made such a nice profit it is only right that they pay the tax? Well, the only problem there is that the profit was not **appreciation** of value but simply **inflation**. In short, the reason they had such a gain was not because their **house** was such a prize, but rather because **all houses** had increased in cost during the thirty years.

Suppose they waited more than the eighteen months to buy a new house. They received a total of $32,000.00 in cash (after taxes).

Sale price	$37,500.00
Commission	-1,875.00
Costs	-400.00
Income Tax	-3,225.00
Net Cash	$32,000.00

I should mention that if the seller is age 65 or over, he may reduce the gain on the sale of a residence (once in a lifetime only), and save some tax dollars. If the sale of such a property is for less than $20,000.00, there will be no tax at all. If the sale price is greater than $20,000.00, the gain will be adjusted according to a formula based on that $20,000.00 exclusion. Beginning in 1977, this sale price basis is increased to $35,000.00.

The moral of this story is simple. If you sell your residence and realize a substantial gain, you should buy a new residence before the eighteen month deadline. You still come out loser (because of the commission and costs of sale), but at least you can put off paying taxes on inflation.

Long term capital gains tax preference is one of the things that makes real estate investment so popular. If you exercise caution, you can make substantial profits, with minimal investments.

Unimproved land is a good example. Ordinarily, such land can be purchased for a very small down payment, frequently ten percent or less. And then, you must make monthly installments on the balance.

As an example, Henry Hauck bought a forty acre parcel

of wooded, mountain land. The purchase price of the land was $16,000.00, and Henry made a down payment of $2,000.00. The owner agreed to carry the balance at 7½ % interest, with payments of $130.00 per month for a fifteen year term.

Henry's parcel was located in an area of reasonable growth. The population had been increasing at the rate of four percent per year for the past five years. His land was within 5 miles of the nearest small town, and within 100 miles of a large, metropolitan city.

The nature of the land and the area more or less guaranteed Henry a profit, or at least no loss. Land has often been called the best hedge against inflation. The logic of this claim is that we are always making more people, but we cannot make more land. Therefore, land will always be in demand, and that demand will always increase.

Armed with the security that his land would hold its value, Henry proceeded to make some income from the land. After waiting the required period to qualify for long term capital gains treatment, he started cutting trees and selling the wood.

Henry was very careful to retain enough trees as to not detract from the land value. He found that he could cut and split two cords of firewood a day.

He bought an old 2½ ton truck for $1,000.00. His chain saws and other equipment cost him $700.00. After he had cut and stacked wood for several weeks, he started looking for a market for his product. He found that local people were willing to pay $50.00 per cord for firewood. He made a contract with a retail wood yard in the large city.

That wood merchant agreed to pay Henry $60.00 per cord for all the firewood Henry could deliver. Since the old truck had a capacity of only three cords, Henry determined that his best deal was to sell as much wood as possible to local people, and then sell the rest to the merchant.

All through the Spring, Summer, and Fall, Henry cut,

split and delivered firewood. When the heavy rains and snow made further work nearly futile, Henry stepped back and assessed his year.

He had harvested 400 cords of firewood from his land, and had sold it for $22,000.00. He had worked very hard for nine months. His expenses of harvesting the wood were as follows: Gasoline, $1,350.00; Oil, $135.00; Truck Repairs, $600.00; Tires, $900.00; Insurance, $200.00; Land Payments, $1,560.00; and Saw Repair, $120.00.

Henry had netted himself more than $17,000.00 for his efforts, and the best is yet to come. Because of a tax loophole that is unique to the timber business, Henry was able to take advantage of long term capital gains on the sale of his wood.

The way the capital gains option works with the sale of timber is as follows: The sale price of the timber is your gross profit; the basis (your cost) is the market value of the standing timber as of January 1 of the year of sale. In this case, the market value of the trees was $2.00 per cord. That was the price that professional firewood cutters were willing to pay for the standing trees, called "stumpage" in the trade.

Since Henry sold 400 cords, his basis was $800.00, leaving him with a long-term capital gain of $21,200.00 on the sale of the wood. The long-term effect of that gain reduced it to $10,600.00. Henry's expenses of doing business came off of that reduced total.

His ordinary income from the wood cutting was zero. The expenses included depreciation, gasoline, oil, repairs, insurance, tires, and interest on the land. The total expenses added up to $5,383.00. The net taxable income was $5,217.00.

Since Henry is a single man, his tax on that income, amounted to $476.00. Without the benefit of this loophole, he would have been liable for a tax of $3,055.00. Henry saved an amazing $2,588.00 in income taxes.

This same rule applies whether Henry cuts the wood himself or hires someone to cut it for him. It also applies to timber used for construction.

SCHEDULE C (Form 1040)

Department of the Treasury
Internal Revenue Service

Profit or (Loss) From Business or Profession

(Sole Proprietorship)

Partnerships, Joint Ventures, etc., Must File Form 1065.

▶ Attach to Form 1040. ▶ See Instructions for Schedule C (Form 1040).

1976

Name of proprietor   HENRY HAUCK

Social security number   789 01 2345

A Principal business activity (see Schedule C Instructions) ▶ SALES ; product ▶ FIREWOOD

B Business name ▶ HENRY'S WOOD SALES   C Employer identification number ▶ N/A

D Business address (number and street) ▶ P.O. BOX AB

City, State and ZIP code ▶ HOLYOKE, VT.

E Indicate method of accounting: (1) ☒ Cash (2) ☐ Accrual (3) ☐ Other ▶

F Were you required to file Form W-3 or Form 1096 for 1976 (see Schedule C Instructions)?

	Yes	No
		X

If "Yes," where filed ▶

G Was an Employer's Quarterly Federal Tax Return, Form 941, filed for this business for any quarter in 1976? ☐ Yes ☒ No

H Method of inventory valuation ▶ .... Was there any substantial change in the manner of determining quantities, costs, or valuations between the opening and closing inventories? (If "Yes," attach explanation) ☐ Yes ☒ No

Income

1 Gross receipts or sales $ .... Less: returns and allowances $ .... Balance ▶	1	— 0 —	
2 Less: Cost of goods sold and/or operations (Schedule C-1, line 8)	2		
3 Gross profit	3		
4 Other income (attach schedule)	4		
5 Total income (add lines 3 and 4)	5	— 0 —	
6 Depreciation (explain in Schedule C-3)	6	333	
7 Taxes on business and business property (explain in Schedule C-2)	7		
8 Rent on business property	8		
9 Repairs (explain in Schedule C-2)	9	720	
10 Salaries and wages not included on line 3, Schedule C-1 (exclude any paid to yourself)	10		
11 Insurance	11	200	
12 Legal and professional fees	12		
13 Commissions	13		
14 Amortization (attach statement)	14		

C

46

Deductions	15 (a) Pension and profit-sharing plans (see Schedule C Instructions)	15(a)	
	(b) Employee benefit programs (see Schedule C Instructions)	(b)	1,045 —
	16 Interest on business indebtedness	16	
	17 Bad debts arising from sales or services	17	
	18 Depletion	18	
	19 Other business expenses (specify):		
	(a) GASOLINE	1,350 —	
	(b) OIL	135 —	
	(c) TIRES	900 —	
	(d) CHAIN SAWS	600 —	
	(e) SMALL TOOLS	100 —	
	(f)		
	(g)		
	(h)		
	(i)		
	(j)		
	(k) Total other business expenses (add lines 19(a) through 19(j))	19(k)	3,085 00
	20 Total deductions (add lines 6 through 19(k))	20	5,383 00

21 Net profit or (loss) (subtract line 20 from line 5). Enter here and on Form 1040, line 29. ALSO enter on Schedule SE, line 5(a). — 21 ⟨5,383 00⟩

SCHEDULE C-1.—Cost of Goods Sold and/or Operations (See Schedule C Instructions for Line 2)

1 Inventory at beginning of year (if different from last year's closing inventory, attach explanation)	1	
2 Purchases $................ Less: cost of items withdrawn for personal use $............ Balance ▶	2	
3 Cost of labor (do not include salary paid to yourself)	3	
4 Materials and supplies	4	
5 Other costs (attach schedule)	5	
6 Total of lines 1 through 5	6	
7 Less: Inventory at end of year	7	
8 Cost of goods sold and/or operations. Enter here and on line 2 above	8	

Did you claim a deduction for expenses of an office in your home? . . . . ☐ Yes ☒ No

Form 4797

Department of the Treasury
Internal Revenue Service

Supplemental Schedule of Gains and Losses

Sales, Exchanges and Involuntary Conversions under
Sections 1231, 1245, 1250, 1251, 1252, and 1254
To be filed with Form 1040, 1041, 1065, 1120, etc.—See Separate Instructions

1976

Name(s) as shown on return

HENRY HAUCK

Identifying number as shown on page 1
of your tax return

789-01-2345

Part I Sales or Exchanges of Property Used in Trade or Business, and Involuntary Conversions (Section 1231)

SECTION A.—Involuntary Conversions Due to Casualty and Theft (See Instruction E)

a. Kind of property (if necessary, attach additional descriptive details not shown below)	b. Date acquired (mo., day, yr.)	c. Date sold (mo., day, yr.)	d. Gross sales price	e. Depreciation allowed (or allowable) since acquisition	f. Cost or other basis, cost of subsequent improvements (if not purchased, attach explanation) and expense of sale	g. Gain or loss (d plus e less f)
1 400 CORDS OAK FIREWOOD	APR '75	OCT '76	22,000 -	- 0 -	800 -	21,200 -
						21,200 -

2 Combine the amounts on line 1. Enter here, and on the appropriate line as follows . . . .
(a) For all except partnership returns:
  (1) If line 2 is zero or a gain, enter such amount in column g, line 3.
  (2) If line 2 is a loss, enter the loss on line 5.
(b) For partnership returns: Enter the amount shown on line 2 above, on Schedule K (Form 1065), line 6.

SECTION B.—Sales or Exchanges of Property Used in Trade or Business and Certain Involuntary Conversions (Not Reportable in Section A) (See Instruction E)

3						21,200 -

4 Combine the amounts on line 3. Enter here, and on the appropriate line as follows . . . . | **21,200 -**

(a) For all except partnership returns:

   (1) If line 4 is a gain, enter such gain as a long-term capital gain on Schedule D (Form 1040, 1120, etc.) that is being filed. See instruction E.

   (2) If line 4 is zero or a loss, enter such amount on line 6.

(b) For partnership returns: Enter the amount shown on line 4 above, on Schedule K (Form 1065), line 7.

▶Part II ◾ Ordinary Gains and Losses

a. Kind of property (if necessary, attach additional descriptive details not shown below)	b. Date acquired (mo., day, yr.)	c. Date sold (mo., day, yr.)	d. Gross sales price	e. Depreciation allowed (or allowable) since acquisition	f. Cost or other basis, cost of subsequent improvements (if not purchased, attach explanation) and expense of sale	g. Gain or loss (d plus e less f)
5 Amount, if any, from line 2(a)(2) .						
6 Amount, if any, from line 4(a)(2) .						
7 Gain, if any, from page 2, line 22						
8						

9 Combine amounts on lines 5 through 8. Enter here, and on the appropriate line as follows

(a) For all except individual returns: Enter the gain or (loss) shown on line 9, on the line provided for on the return (Form 1120, etc.) being filed. See instruction F for specific line reference.

(b) For individual returns:

   (1) If the gain or (loss) on line 9, includes losses which are to be treated as an itemized deduction on Schedule A (Form 1040) (see instruction F), enter the total of such loss(es) here and include on Schedule A (Form 1040), line 29—identify as "loss from Form 4797, line 9(b)(1)". . . . .

   (2) Redetermine the gain or (loss) on line 9, excluding the loss (if any) entered on line 9(b)(1). Enter here and on Form 1040, line 31 . . . .

Form **4797** (1976)

49

Let's carry Henry's situation a little further. In one year, he has removed 400 cords of firewood from a 40 acre parcel of land. Keeping in mind his early decision that he would not ruin the value of the land by taking out too many trees, you must realize that his parcel was indeed heavily wooded. Even so, at the end of such an active year, there would be very little firewood remaining.

Henry anticipated this problem. In May, right during his woodcutting, he made a down payment on another, larger parcel of land. This time, he found a quarter section (160 acres), with an abundance of firewood, along with a good stand of pine trees, ready for the sawmill. His down payment of $4,500.00 on a total price of $48,000.00 left him with payments of $375.00 per month.

As soon as his woodcutting season ended, he put the original parcel on the market, asking a price of $17,500.00. He sold very soon, and after paying the expenses of the sale, realized a slight profit (about $500.00), which qualified as long-term capital gains. But more important, it gave him $3,000.00 in cash. The burden of the heavy, double land payments had left him a little short of cash.

The following year, Henry would contract with loggers to cut the stand of pine trees. As part of the deal, they would develop roads throughout his 160 acre parcel. When the weather broke, he began his firewood cutting again, but this time he had more than just a one year supply. His income from the sale of the pine logs as well as the firewood, was long-term capital gains. He received $6,000.00 from the logs without lifting a finger.

The total income from the new year will be $27,000.00, half of which is taxable. The total tax bill will be somewhere in the neighborhood of $1,300.00. Henry's actual, after tax income will be just under $20,000.00.

If he continues along with his plan of action, he should be able to combine high earnings, hard work, and low taxes for a long, long time. And with luck, somewhere along the way, he might be able to cut back on the amount of his own labor by hiring a strong backed young man to help him.

Chapter 6

Rental Property

Rental property: what it means to your current income tax picture. The investment potential of rental property. A complete example of the expenses and tax shelters available in rentals. Depreciation and taxes: a further reduction. Rental property as a retirement home or investment. Restrictions imposed on vacation rental property by the Tax Reform Act of 1976. Examples of rental property expenses and allowable deductions related to this type of property with cash flow charts and income tax effects. Apartment and motel properties with examples of tax deductions on these types of investments.

One of the most popular ways to invest money with the idea of reducing taxes is through the purchase and maintenance of rental property. This is no gimmick. It is one of the best methods of investment that I can recommend. Rental property can accomplish several things for you. First, it can shelter a portion of your ordinary income. Second, it can provide you with a hedge against inflation. Third, if properly managed, it can provide you with a nice retirement income.

John Smith is a machinist for a large company. He earns about $20,000.00 annually in his employment. He is thirty-eight years old, married, and has three children, all in school. He owns his own home outright, and has $6,000.00 savings in the bank.

John's income puts him in a 28% tax bracket. This year, he will not have enough legal deductions to itemize (his house is paid for, so there is no mortgage interest). He will have to take the standard deduction, and his tax will be $2,860.00.

If John purchases a rental house, the effect could be substantial. Let's assume John searches until he finds a sound house in a fairly good neighborhood. He makes a down payment of $5,000.00 on the purchase price of $30,000.00. He is now the proud owner of a rental property. The terms of repayment for the remaining $25,000.00 are as follows: John will repay $200.00 per month for the next twenty-five years, at 8½% interest. In addition, he will also be obligated to pay $500.00 annual property taxes, and he must maintain the house in good order.

A general rule of thumb for rental property is that the rental income should be 10% of the purchase price. In this case, John chooses to rent the house for $275.00 per month. His reason is that he hopes to attract a more permanent renter by offering the lower rate. This more permanent renter would logically take better care of the house and property, and result in lower maintenance costs for John, as well as a lower vacancy rate.

And the $275.00 per month income will cover John's cash flow. His fixed costs include the $200.00 payment, plus $42.00 set aside for the payment of property taxes. This leaves him $33.00 per month to set aside for repairs and maintenance.

With his monthly "cash flow" under control, let's take a look at the annual figures. Normally, income from rental property should be reduced by a "vacancy factor." With the incentive of a reduced rental rate, John hopes to keep this vacancy factor at a minimum, somewhere around the 5% level. If we reduce the $3,300.00 maximum annual income by $165.00, we are left with $3,135.00. This is our basis for projected annual income.

The fixed expense includes $2,400.00 in payments, plus $500.00 property taxes and insurance of $50.00. Add to this the estimated variable costs for repair and maintenance of $240.00 ($20.00 x 12 months). If the rental is occupied all year, the net is a $110.00, but taking the vacancy factor into consideration means an annual cash loss of $55.00.

INCOME	$3,135.00
PAYMENTS	-2,400.00
INSURANCE	-50.00
TAXES	-500.00
REPAIRS	-240.00
LOSS	-55.00

Now, you might say, a loss of $55.00 per year is not too good. However, there is more to it than meets the eye. When John fills out his income tax return, he will recoup that $55.00 and more.

In addition to the $500.00 tax expense, John also has other deductions that he can claim against his rental property. For instance, he will pay interest of $2,110.00 in the first year. He sets up the depreciation of the house on a thirty five year life, and depreciates it on a 150% declining balance. Since the cost was $30,000.00, the depreciation for one year is $1,286.00.

John is also entitled to claim certain other expenses related to the rental property. Since he is a landlord, and on call for any repairs that might be needed, he can claim the expense of his telephone, or at least a portion of his telephone expense. Also, he can claim any and all of his expenses incurred in traveling to the rental property to inspect his investment.

SCHEDULE E
(Form 1040)

Department of the Treasury
Internal Revenue Service

Supplemental Income Schedule

1976

(From pensions and annuities, rents and royalties, partnerships, estates and trusts, etc.)

▶ Attach to Form 1040.　　▶ See Instructions for Schedule E (Form 1040).

Name(s) as shown on Form 1040　**JOHN SMITH**

Your social security number
123 45 6789

Part I　Pension and Annuity Income.
If fully taxable, do not complete this part. Enter amount on Form 1040, line 32b. For one pension or annuity not fully taxable, complete this part. If you have more than one pension or annuity that is not fully taxable, attach a schedule and enter combined total of taxable portions on line 5.

1 Name of payer .			
2 Did your employer contribute part of the cost?			☐ Yes ☐ No
If "Yes," is your contribution recoverable within 3 years of the annuity starting date? . .			☐ Yes ☐ No
If "Yes," show: Your contribution $............., Contribution recovered in prior years		2	
3 Amount received this year		3	
4 Amount excludable this year		4	
5 Taxable portion (subtract line 4 from line 3)			5

Part II　Rent and Royalty Income.
If you need more space, use Form 4831.

Have you claimed expenses connected with your vacation home rented to others? . ☐ Yes ☐ No

Note: If you are reporting farm rental income here, see Schedule E Instructions to determine if you should file Form 4835. If at least two-thirds of your gross income is from farming or fishing, check this box ▶ ☐.

(a) Kind and location of property If residential, also write "R"	(b) Total amount of rents	(c) Total amount of royalties	(d) Depreciation (explain below) or depletion (attach computation)	(e) Other expenses (Repairs, etc.— explain below)
RESIDENCE 2305 DAISY DRIVE PRINCETON, N.J.	3135–		1286–	2954–
6 Totals	3135–		1286–	2954–

7 Net income or (loss) from rents and royalties (column (b) plus column (c) less columns (d) and (e)) . .	7		〈1105–〉
8 Net rental income or (loss) (from Form 4831)	8		
9 Net farm rental profit or (loss) (from Form 4835)	9		
10 Total rent and royalty income (add lines 7, 8, and 9)		10	〈1105–〉

Part III Income or Losses from Partnerships, Estates or Trusts, Small Business Corporations.

Note: If any of the partnership, estate or trust income reported below is from farming or fishing, see Schedule E Instructions to determine if you should also file Form 4835. If at least two-thirds of your gross income is from farming or fishing, check this box ▶ ☐.

Enter in column (b): P for Partnership, E for Estate or Trust, or S for Small Business Corp.

(a) Name	(b)	(c) Employer identification number	(d) Income or (loss)	(e) Additional 1st year depreciation (applicable only to partnerships)

11 Totals

12 Income or (loss). Total of column (d) less total of column (e) . . . . | 12

13 TOTAL (add lines 5, 10, and 12). Enter here and on Form 1040, line 32a . . . ▶ | 13 | ‹1105-›

Explanation of Column (e), Part II

Item	Amount	Item	Amount
INTEREST	2,110-	TRAVEL	18-
TAXES	500-	INSURANCE	50-
REPAIRS	216-		
TELEPHONE	60-		

Schedule for Depreciation Claimed in Part II Above
If you need more space use Form 4562.

(a) Description of property	(b) Date acquired	(c) Cost or other basis	(d) Depreciation allowed or allowable in prior years	(e) Method of computing depreciation	(f) Life or rate	(g) Depreciation for this year
1 Total additional first-year depreciation (do not include in items below)						
FRAME HOUSE	1976	30,600-	-0-	150 DB	35	1286-
2 Totals		30,000-				1286-

Income		$3,135.00
Expenses		
Interest	$2,110.00	
Taxes	500.00	
Repairs	216.00	
Telephone	60.00	
Travel at		
15 cents		
per mile	18.00	
Insurance	50.00	
	$2,954.00	
Depreciation	1,286.00	
		$4,240.00
Net Loss		-$1,105.00

In John's tax bracket, the loss of $1,105.00 means a reduction in his taxes of $309.40, leaving him with a net annual profit of $254.40 actual cash.

You may say, "So what? That's not much pay for the effort involved in being a landlord." Of course, you are right. The true benefit of such a rental property will not be seen for years.

Look at it this way—How many retirement plans can you think of right off hand that PAY YOU in the years **before** retirement? At the end of the twenty-five year mortgage, John will be sixty-three years old, and he will very likely be ready to retire.

At that time, his cash flow will look like this (in 1976 dollars):

INCOME	$3,135.00
INSURANCE	50.00
TAXES	500.00
REPAIRS	240.00
PROFIT	$2,345.00

That amounts to about a $200.00 monthly supplement to his Social Security, and in effect it did not cost him anything but his effort.

Many people use the rental property loophole to obtain a retirement home, also. By purchasing a home in the area in which they plan to retire, and holding it as a rental until they are ready, they can have their cake and eat it, too.

Commonly, such a retirement property is located in a vacation or holiday region. In such a case, the owners might elect to rent the house to vacationers on a daily or weekly basis. They can also use the house, within limits, for their own vacations.

The Tax Reform Act of 1976 spells out the restrictions for such a vacation rental property. If you use the house personally for more than two weeks a year, or for more than 10% of the days that you rent it out, you cannot deduct more for maintenance, depreciation, and utilities than the total amount of rental income minus such customary deductions as property taxes and interest. If you rent the house for less than 15 days, you do not have to report the income . . . but you cannot get the "extra" deductions.

Here is an example:

George Everyman has a home located in a popular mountain resort area. He lives in a city about 200 miles from this area, and likes to visit his vacation retreat whenever possible. However, in order to offset the expenses of such a home, he offers it for rent to others.

George realizes the inconvenience of trying to take care of the details of rental from his distant location. He has signed an agreement with a real estate agency in the resort area to act as his agent. For a fee, the agency advertises George's house, collects the rent, inspects the premises, and oversees necessary repairs to the property.

Because the house is located in such a popular resort area, George is able to ask for and receive a high rental rate. He charges $35.00 daily rent, and also offers a weekly rate of $175.00. During the summer months, the house is almost always rented. His income for that period is normally in the neighborhood of $1800.00. During the remainder of the year, the house is rented about 50% of the time, for an income of $3,500.00.

His total annual income from the rental is usually somewhere near $5,300.00. And that represents a total rental time of 212 days. That, in turn, means that George

SCHEDULE E
(Form 1040)

Department of the Treasury
Internal Revenue Service

Supplemental Income Schedule

(From pensions and annuities, rents and royalties, partnerships, estates and trusts, etc.)

▶ Attach to Form 1040. ▶ See Instructions for Schedule E (Form 1040).

1976

Name(s) as shown on Form 1040
GEORGE EVERYMAN

Your social security number
876 : 54 : 3210

Part I — Pension and Annuity Income.

If fully taxable, do not complete this part. Enter amount on Form 1040, line 32b. For one pension or annuity not fully taxable, complete this part. If you have more than one pension or annuity that is not fully taxable, attach a schedule and enter combined total of taxable portions on line 5.

1 Name of payer		
2 Did your employer contribute part of the cost?	☐ Yes ☐ No	
If "Yes," is your contribution recoverable within 3 years of the annuity starting date? . . .	☐ Yes ☐ No	
If "Yes," show: Your contribution $............ Contribution recovered in prior years	2	
3 Amount received this year	3	
4 Amount excludable this year	4	
5 Taxable portion (subtract line 4 from line 3)	5	

Part II — Rent and Royalty Income.

If you need more space, use Form 4831.

Have you claimed expenses connected with your vacation home rented to others? . ☐ Yes ☐ No

Note: If you are reporting farm rental income here, see Schedule E Instructions to determine if you should file Form 4835. If at least two-thirds of your gross income is from farming or fishing, check this box ▶ ☐.

(a) Kind and location of property If residential, also write "R"	(b) Total amount of rents	(c) Total amount of royalties	(d) Depreciation (explain below) or depletion (attach computation)	(e) Other expenses (Repairs, etc.— explain below)
FRAME HOUSE (R) LAKE TAHOE, NEV.	5300.-		1250.-	6521.-

6 Totals	5300.-		1250.-	6521.-	
7 Net income or (loss) from rents and royalties (column (b) plus column (c) less columns (d) and (e)) .			7	⟨2471.-⟩	
8 Net rental income or (loss) (from Form 4831)			8		
9 Net farm rental profit or (loss) (from Form 4835)			9		
10 Total rent and royalty income (add lines 7, 8, and 9)			10	⟨2471.-⟩	

58

Part III Income or Losses from Partnerships, Estates or Trusts, Small Business Corporations.

Note: If any of the partnership, estate or trust income reported below is from farming or fishing, see Schedule E Instructions to determine if you should also file Form 4835. If at least two-thirds of your gross income is from farming or fishing, check this box ▶ ☐

Enter in column (b): P for Partnership, E for Estate or Trust, or S for Small Business Corp.

(a) Name	(b)	(c) Employer identification number	(d) Income or (loss)	(e) Additional 1st year depreciation (applicable only to partnerships)

11 Totals

12 Income or (loss). Total of column (d) less total of column (e) 12

13 TOTAL (add lines 5, 10, and 12). Enter here and on Form 1040, line 32a . . . . . . ▶ 13 ⎰2471 -⎱

Explanation of Column (e), Part II

Item	Amount		Item	Amount
INTEREST	3573 -	UTILITIES		600 -
TAXES	600 -	MGT. FEES		530 -
INSURANCE	300 -	TRAVEL		60 -
REPAIRS	300 -	HOME OFFICE		558 -

Schedule for Depreciation Claimed in Part II Above
If you need more space use Form 4562.

(a) Description of property	(b) Date acquired	(c) Cost or other basis	(d) Depreciation allowed or allowable in prior years	(e) Method of computing depreciation	(f) Life or rate	(g) Depreciation for this year
1 Total additional first-year depreciation (do not include in items below)						E
FRAME HOUSE	1976	50,000 -	- 0 -	SL	40	1,250 -
2 Totals		50,000 -				1,250 -

can use the house for twenty-one days during the year, without any loss of deductions.

George has a fifteen-year mortgage, at 9% interest, for the balance of $40,000.00 on the house. His payments are $400.00 per month. The property taxes on the house are $600.00 each year. Due to the fact that the house is located in an area where fire risk is great, and also because he wishes to have extensive liability coverage, his insurance premium is a relatively high $300.00 annually.

He estimates his repairs at about 6% annually, and sets aside this amount. If he does not use the whole amount in any given year, he leaves it in a special bank account set aside for this purpose, and adds to it the following year.

The real estate agency charges a fee amounting to 10% of the total rental income. The utilities average $50.00 per month over the year, or $600.00 per year.

```
    INCOME ...................... $5,300.00
        PAYMENTS        $4,800.00
        TAXES              600.00
        INSURANCE          300.00
        REPAIRS            300.00
        UTILITIES          600.00
        FEES               530.00_____
    NET ........................ -$1,830.00
```

As you can see, the annual cash flow indicates a loss of $1,830.00 per year. However, that is offset by the tax effect, and also by the vacation benefit that George and his family receive.

Now, since George was careful not to exceed the 10% residency limitation (21 days in this case), he is entitled to take full advantage of all the deductions that normally go along with any rental property.

In addition to those shown on the cash flow chart, he is also entitled to deductions for depreciation, and other expenses. If he had exceeded the 21 day limitation, he could only claim deductions for the interest and property taxes he paid.

George paid $50,000.00 for the house, and it was a newly constructed residence. He should put the house on a forty-year depreciation schedule, and on a straight-line basis. The depreciation for the first year if $1,250.00. In addition to this deduction, he is entitled to deductions for travel between his home and the rental property.

As a landlord, it is prudent for him to personally inspect his property on a periodic basis. Since he has retained the real estate agency, his inspection visits would logically be limited. It seems reasonable that he should make two or three visits per year for that purpose. Also, a portion of his home can be designated as an office, and certain telephone expenses related to the property can be deducted. Since the one-way mileage between his home and the rental is 200 miles, George can claim a travel expense of $60.00 for each "inspection" visit (400 round-trip miles at 15 cents per mile).

George has set aside one room in his 7 room house as an office. Since this "home office" is the principal place of business for George's rental enterprise, he is entitled to claim deductions for expenses at his home. He can take depreciation on 1/7 of the value of his home, and he can claim 1/7 of the expense of such normal living expenses as utilities, insurance, and heating of his home.

He can claim all telephone expenses that are directly tied to the rental property, plus 1/7 of his basic monthly charge. The reason he is entitled to these deductions is that as landlord, he is on call at any time, concerning the property.

Now, a bit of information on George. He is a successful businessman, with an annual income of $26,000.00 per year. He is married, and has two children. His itemized deductions average $4,000.00 each year. His tax, without the rental property, would be $4,100.00, and his highest tax bracket is 28%.

With the rental, his tax will be $3,408.00, a saving of $692.00. That cuts his cash loss down from $1,830.00 to $1,138.00. Add to that tax saving the money he saves by not having to rent a vacation house, and he comes out even better. We could assume that George would normally take two weeks vacation, at a rental cost of $210.00, making a total saving of $560.00. This further reduces his cash loss to $578.00, or about $48.00 per month.

Remember now, that George's mortgage will be paid in fifteen years. After that, his cash flow will do an about face. Instead of a $1,830.00 loss, he will show a profit of about $3,000.00 (some of which will be taxable).

More specifically, his net income (taxable) will be $1,100.00, and the tax effect will be $300.00. That "extra" income tax will reduce his actual cash income to $2,700.00 per year, plus the vacation value.

Over the period of the fifteen year mortgage, George's total out of pocket expense will add up to $8,670.00. It will take him only three years to recoup those losses. And in another five years, he will have recovered his original down payment. The net result is marvelous . . . George will have a beautiful retirement home, located in his favorite place in the world, and it didn't cost him anything.

Other examples of rental property investments are hotels, motels, and apartments. These properties require substantially more investment of cash and time, but they can be as good or better than the individual residence examples above.

Sam Smith is a self-employed building contractor. He earns about $50,000.00 each year in his business, and has accumulated savings of $60,000.00 over the past several years. In addition to his own thrift, he inherited $25,000.00 from the estate of his late mother, for a total of $85,000.00 in the bank, earning seven percent interest per year.

Sam uses $70,000.00 of his savings to make a down payment on a twenty unit apartment complex. The total price of this apartment building is $300,000.00, and the previous owner is carrying the mortgage balance of $230,000.00 at 7½ percent interest, with payments of $2,000.00 per month for 16 years.

When all of the apartments are occupied, the rental income is $3,450.00 per month. However, due to the nature of this type of rental property, full occupancy is seldom accomplished. For budgetting purposes, Sam has calculated in a ten percent vacancy factor. This brings the monthly income total down to $3,100.00.

In addition to his monthly payment to the previous owner, Sam must also budget for other expenses. He calculates that his repair expense will be $300.00 per month, and that his insurance will be $1,800.00 annually, or $150.00 per month.

His property taxes amount to $3,300.00 per year, so Sam puts $275.00 each month in a special account for the purpose of paying those taxes. Since there is nearly always a vacancy, he must advertise in a local newspaper, at a cost of $40.00 per month.

His cash flow looks like this:

```
INCOME ...................  $3,100.00
     PAYMENTS       2,000.00
     REPAIRS          300.00
     INSURANCE        150.00
     TAXES            275.00
     ADVERTISING       40.00
  NET ......................  $  335.00
```

A cash return of $335.00 per month on an investment of $70,000.00 represents a percentage yield of 5.7%, somewhat less than the bank was paying. The tax effect of this transaction is profound, however, and the actual yield is much greater than 7%.

You will recall that Sam's earnings from his business is $50,000.00 per year, and that is after his business expenses. Without the apartment building investment, Sam's tax bill for the year would be $12,140.00.

The tax effect on the apartment looks like this:

INCOME		$37,200.00
EXPENSES		
Repairs	$3,600.00	
Insurance	1,800.00	
Taxes	3,300.00	
Advertising	480.00	
Interest	17,100.00	
Total Expenses	26,280.00	
Depreciation	11,250.00	
TOTAL EXPENSES		37,530.00
NET TAXABLE INCOME		($330.00)

In Sam's tax bracket, that slight loss (which is only on paper), will save him $110.00 in federal income tax. When you add the $110.00 to the $4,020.00 ($335.00 x 12 months) that he gains in cash each year, it brings the percentage yield on his original investment of $70,000.00 up to 5.9%. The figure that you must compare this with is the 7% that was being paid by the bank. That bank interest paid $4,900.00 each year, but all of that was taxable. After paying taxes on the interest, Sam would be left with only $2,548.00, or a percentage yield of only 3.6%.

When you consider all these things along with the gain in equity that Sam is achieving, it becomes evident that this apartment investment is a very wise one for him. The obvious drawback is the large capital investment required, and it should be mentioned that Sam, being a building contractor, is able to do many of his own repairs.

Just briefly, we should mention motel and hotel investment in this chapter. Since this type of investment is more frequently combined with self employment, it will be covered from that aspect in the chapter on being in business. However, some people buy motels and hotels with no intention of taking active part in the management.

Ordinarily, the same income and expense rules apply to this type of investment that we found in the apartment or single residence examples, with one notable exception: The primary objective of motel and hotel investment is **not** income during the period of ownership, but rather the capital gains that come at the sale of the property.

Because of tax benefits that are unique to this business, it is possible to substantially avoid paying **any** taxes at all on the gain realized from the sale of such property. The trick is to re-invest into another motel or hotel.

Motels and hotels are intended for transient renters, rather than permanent renters. That fact alone makes them eligible for an investment credit of 10% of the purchase price. That credit is applied to any tax liability in the year of purchase, but even if your tax is less than the amount of the credit, you do not lose the remainder of the credit. It can be carried back against taxes paid in the prior three years, and any remainder after that can be carried forward against taxes you owe in the next five years. This investment credit will be explained more thoroughly in another chapter.

Chapter 7

Self-Employment

Self-employment: whether vocation or avocation calls for special tax techniques and allows special advantages. Examples of the small business tax preparation. What you deduct as business expenses including depreciation, tools and equipment and insurance. Examples of depreciation rates. Promotional entertainment deductions you can use. The Investment Tax Credit: how to make the dollars you invest in your business assets work twice. An example of using this credit to pyramid your capital. Self-employment taxes: a deductible way toward retirement.

Ah, the joys and sorrows of being your own boss. The pride of knowing that your accomplishments will be recognized and will benefit you directly . . . the anguish of knowing that you must personally suffer the penalties of your errors.

When you work for someone else, and you do a particularly good job, about all you can hope for is a pat on the back, or maybe a little something extra in your paycheck. But the old saying is, "You will never get rich working for someone else." And it has a ring of truth, because your employer will reap the rewards of your effort. And he will get to take advantage of the many tax loopholes available to the self employed.

These loopholes are available to anyone who ventures to start a business, whether large or small. They range from depreciation to business entertainment, and they are there for the taking.

A small business can be anything from a home sewing and clothing business to driving a hard-top racer at the local dirt track on Saturday night. It can be as small as you wish, or as large as you can handle. It can be your major source of income, or can be a sideline business. You can convert a hobby or avocation to a business status, and write off many expenses.

We will look at some examples of self employment, large and small. You will see how the loopholes open up and how to take advantage of them.

John Adams, is an electrician. He is employed full time by an electrical contractor to do electrical installation in homes and commercial buildings. John has a part time business, operated out of the converted garage of his home. In this business, he repairs televisions, stereo systems, radios, and small appliances. His first love, though, is designing and building custom stereophonic music systems.

The garage of John's home, when purchased, had a value of $2,400.00. He spent another $1,200.00 to remodel the garage into a shop suitable for his work. Thus he has a $3,600.00 basis for depreciation on that part of his residence. He bought a pickup for the business for $4,667.00. He purchased scopes, guages and tools for his trade at a cost of $3,500.00. He can also take depreciation on these.

John earns $14,000.00 per year working for wages. He is married, and has three children. He lives in a small town in the midwest. His wages, less his itemized deductions, put him in a 19% tax bracket. Without the loopholes of his side-line business, his tax would be $1,190.00.

John is not especially interested in making a lot of

money with his business. His primary direction is toward developing new stereo ideas. He does enough repair work to keep him supplied with parts and materials. His gross income for the year from the business is $3,500.00. (See tax forms on following page).

Now this loss of $2,035.00 is what John reports on his tax return, but it is not the actual cash situation. His income of $3,500.00 is true, as is the cost of materials of $720.00.

But his out of pocket expenses are only as follows: $360.00 for the repairs to his pickup truck; $50.00 for pickup insurance; $60.00 advertising; $120.00 promotional entertainment; the $240.00 auto expense for the pickup. The total cash out of pocket, including the cost of materials, is $1,550.00, leaving John with a cash surplus of $1,950.00.

The other deductions are either on paper, or are expenses that would have been incurred anyway, but would not have been deductible without the business.

The depreciation is as follows: Since John purchased the pickup and the equipment this year, he is entitled to a special, first-year, bonus depreciation, 20% of the purchase price. He does not claim any bonus depreciation on the garage, or on the remodeling expenses. He takes depreciation on the shop, based on the $3,600.00 value, on a twenty year life, using the 125% of declining balance method. That is, he divides the value by the 20-year life, and then multiplies the result by 125%.

The tools and equipment are depreciated over a seven year period, using $3,000.00 as the basis ($3,500.00 cost, minus $500.00 taken as the 20% bonus) and using the 200% declining balance method. The pickup truck is depreciated over a five year life, with $4,000.00 as the basis after the 20% effect, and also using the 200% method.

John's shop makes up approximately one seventh of the total space of his home. That 1/7 fraction is used in allocating the expenses of insurance, part of the interest, and utilities. In fact, one-seventh of just about all of his household maintenance can be charged to the business.

The obvious exceptions might be a back yard patio or bedroom furniture. You will note that although only one-seventh of the mortgage interest was applied as business expense, John does not necessarily lose the remainder. The balance of the interest can be carried as an itemized deduction.

John's home insurance runs $100.00 per year. The 1/7 fraction gives him a deduction of $14.00 (which was added to the $50.00 pickup insurance). His utilities run about $50.00 per month, or $600.00 per year, so the business portion is $86.00. The $50.00 telephone is the basic monthly rate, since John has listed his phone under the business name.

The $120.00 spent on promotional entertainment is spent. Instead of just going out for an evening, John now invites a customer to go along, and pays the expenses of the customer. Note: Your guest for entertainment does not need to be an existing customer. He can be a **prospective** customer, or someone who supplies merchandise to you. the requirement is that the expense must be **primarily** for the promotion of business. Another note of interest: If the total expenses do not exceed $25.00 for any one case, you do not need to keep receipts. All you need is a written record (sort of like a diary), showing the date, the amount, who you entertained, his business connection, and what was discussed.

Now, John had a cash surplus of $1,950.00, and showed a tax loss of $2,035.00. Let's take a look at the tax effect of the business loss.

John can reduce his adjusted gross income by the $2,035.00. From the $14,000.00 to $11,965.00. His itemized deductions, which totalled $3,250.00 before figuring the business expenses, have changed. Since he has listed one-seventh of his mortgage interest as a business expense, he can claim only the remaining six-sevenths as an itemized deduction. This action reduces his itemized interest deduction by $386.00.

However, since his adjusted gross income was reduced by $2,035.00, the 3% effect on his medical expenses is

SCHEDULE C (Form 1040)

Department of the Treasury
Internal Revenue Service

Profit or (Loss) From Business or Profession

(Sole Proprietorship)

Partnerships, Joint Ventures, etc., Must File Form 1065.

▶ Attach to Form 1040. ▶ See Instructions for Schedule C (Form 1040).

1976

Name of proprietor **JOHN ADAMS**

Social security number **123 45 6789**

A Principal business activity (see Schedule C Instructions) ▶ **SERVICE** ....; product ▶ **ELECTRICAL REPAIR**

B Business name ▶ **JOHN'S FIXIT SHOP** .... C Employer identification number ▶ **N/A**

D Business address (number and street) ▶ **123 PEACH ST.**

City, State and ZIP code ▶ **FRUITRIDGE, PA**

E Indicate method of accounting: (1) ☒ Cash (2) ☐ Accrual (3) ☐ Other ▶

	Yes	No
F Were you required to file Form W-3 or Form 1096 for 1976 (see Schedule C Instructions)?		X
If "Yes," where filed ▶		
G Was an Employer's Quarterly Federal Tax Return, Form 941, filed for this business for any quarter in 1976?		X
H Method of inventory valuation ▶ **FIFO** ...... Was there any substantial change in the manner of determining quantities, costs, or valuations between the opening and closing inventories? (If "Yes," attach explanation)		X

Income

1 Gross receipts or sales $ **1850—** Less: returns and allowances $ **—0—** Balance ▶	1	1850 00
2 Less: Cost of goods sold and/or operations (Schedule C-1, line 8)	2	720 00
3 Gross profit	3	1130 00
4 Other income (attach schedule) **REPAIR LABOR**	4	1650 00
5 Total income (add lines 3 and 4)	5	2780 00
6 Depreciation (explain in Schedule C-3)	6	3449 00
7 Taxes on business and business property (explain in Schedule C-2)	7	
8 Rent on business property	8	
9 Repairs (explain in Schedule C-2)	9	360 00
10 Salaries and wages not included on line 3, Schedule C-1 (exclude any paid to yourself)	10	
11 Insurance	11	64 00
12 Legal and professional fees	12	
13 Commissions	13	
14 Amortization (attach statement)	14	

Deductions

15 (a) Pension and profit-sharing plans (see Schedule C Instructions)		15(a)	
(b) Employee benefit programs (see Schedule C Instructions)		(b)	
16 Interest on business indebtedness		16	386 00
17 Bad debts arising from sales or services		17	
18 Depletion		18	
19 Other business expenses (specify):			
(a) ADVERTISING	60 00		
(b) UTILITIES	86 00		
(c) TELEPHONE	50 00		
(d) BUSINESS PROMOTION	120 90		
(e) AUTO (GAS, OIL, TIRES)	240 00		
(f)			
(g)			
(h)			
(i)			
(j)			
(k) Total other business expenses (add lines 19(a) through 19(j))		19(k)	556 60
20 Total deductions (add lines 6 through 19(k))		20	4815 00

21 Net profit or (loss) (subtract line 20 from line 5). Enter here and on Form 1040, line 29. ALSO enter on Schedule SE, line 5(a).   **21** ⟨2035 00⟩

SCHEDULE C-1.—Cost of Goods Sold and/or Operations (See Schedule C Instructions for Line 2)

1 Inventory at beginning of year (if different from last year's closing inventory, attach explanation)	1	-0-
2 Purchases $ 1,000 - Less: cost of items withdrawn for personal use $ 280 - Balance ▶	2	720 00
3 Cost of labor (do not include salary paid to yourself)	3	-0-
4 Materials and supplies	4	-0-
5 Other costs (attach schedule)	5	-0-
6 Total of lines 1 through 5	6	720 00
7 Less: Inventory at end of year	7	-0-
8 Cost of goods sold and/or operations. Enter here and on line 2 above	8	720 00

Did you claim a deduction for expenses of an office in your home?   ☐ Yes ☒ No

Form **3468**	**Computation of Investment Credit**		19**76**
Department of the Treasury Internal Revenue Service	▶ Attach to your tax return.		

Name **John Adams**

Identifying number as shown on page 1 of your tax return **123-45-6789**

1 Use schedule below to list qualified investment in new and used property acquired or constructed and placed in service during the taxable year; and also list qualified progress expenditures made during the 1976 taxable year and qualified progress expenditures made in 1974 and 1975 taxable years providing a proper election as prescribed in section 46(d)(6) was made for such prior years. If progress expenditure property is placed in service during the taxable year, do not list qualified progress expenditures for this property. See Specific Instruction for line 1.

If 100% investment credit is being claimed on certain ships, check this block. ▶ ☐ See Instruction K for details.

Note: *Include your share of investment in property made by a partnership, estate, trust, small business corporation, or lessor.*

Type of property	Line	(1) Life years	(2) Cost or basis (See instruction G)	(3) Applicable percentage	(4) Qualified investment (Column 2 x column 3)
New property	(a)	3 or more but less than 5		33⅓	
	(b)	5 or more but less than 7	4,667.00	66⅔	3,111.00
	(c)	7 or more	3,500.00	100	3,500.00
Qualified progress expenditures — 1974 and 1975	(d)	7 or more		20	
1976	(e)	7 or more		40	
Used property (See instructions for dollar limitation)	(f)	3 or more but less than 5		33⅓	
	(g)	5 or more but less than 7		66⅔	
	(h)	7 or more		100	

2 Qualified investment—add lines 1(a) thru (h)		6611.00
3 10% of line 2		661.10
4 7% (4% for public utility property) of certain property (see Instruction for line 1)		
5 Electing corporations with qualifying stock ownership plans—Enter 1% of line 2 (see Instruction I). (Attach election statement.)		
6 Carryback and carryover of unused credit(s). See instruction F—attach computation		
7 Tentative investment credit—Add lines 3, 4, 5 and 6		661 —

72

Limitation

8
 (a) Individuals—Enter amount from line 18, page 1, Form 1040 . . . . ⎫
 (b) Estates and trusts—Enter amount from line 24 or 25, page 1, Form 1041 . . . . . ⎬   865-
 (c) Corporations—Enter amount from line 9, Schedule J, page 3, Form 1120 . . . . . ⎭

9 Less: **(a)** Credit for the elderly (individuals only) . . . .
 (b) Foreign tax credit . . . . . .
 (c) Tax on lump-sum distributions (see instruction for line 9(c)) . . .
 (d) Possession Tax Credit (corporations only) . . . .   -0-

10 Total—Add lines 9(a), (b), (c) and (d)   865-

11 Line 8 less line 10   865-

12 (a) Enter amount on line 11 or $25,000, whichever is lesser. (Married persons filing separately, controlled corporate groups, estates, and trusts, see instruction for line 12.) . . . .
 (b) If line 11 exceeds line 12(a), enter 50% of the excess. (Public utilities, railroads, and airlines see instruction J.)   865-

13 Total—Add lines 12(a) and (b)   661-

14 Investment credit—Amount from line 7 or line 13, whichever is lesser. Enter here and on line 50, Form 1040; line 10(b), Schedule J, page 3, Form 1120; or the appropriate line on other returns . . . .

Schedule A
If any part of your investment in line 1 or 4 above was made by a partnership, estate, trust, small business corporation, or lessor, complete the following statement and identify property qualifying for the 7% or 10% investment credit.

Name (Partnership, estate, trust, etc.)	Address	Progress expenditures	New	Used	Life years
				Property	
		$	$	$	

If property is disposed of prior to the life years used in computing the investment credit, see instruction E.

73

also reduced. Three percent of $2,035.00 is $61.05, and his itemized medical expenses increase by that amount.

After deducting for what's left of his itemized deductions, and after further deducting $3,750.00 for his exemptions ($750.00 each for himself, his wife, and the three children), John is left with a taxable income of $5,290.00. The tax on that amount is $865.00, a savings of $325.00 over the prior calculation without the business.

Pretty good, you say? Brother, you ain't seen nothing yet. Since he is an enterprising businessman, and invests much of his capital in improvements, he is entitled to take advantage of the Investment Tax Credit. His capital improvements of tools and equipment, including the pickup truck, qualify for this magical tax loophole.

The investment credit is an income tax loophole granted to taxpayers engaged in business or who hold property for the production of income. It applies to machinery, equipment, and other tangible, depreciable property. The property can be either new or used, and it must have a depreciation life of three years or more. Property held for seven years or more qualifies for the maximum credit.

As a general rule, buildings do **not** qualify for the investment credit, nor do improvements made to buildings. The exceptions are new elevators and escalators in buildings. The only buildings or structures that qualify entirely are hotels and motels that are used predominantly by transients. We will discuss these exceptions later in this chapter.

In John's case, he purchased a pickup truck for a price of $4,667.00, and depreciated it over a five-year period. That means two-thirds of the truck investment, or $3,111.00, qualifies for investment credit. Since he is depreciating his tools and equipment over a seven year period, the entire $3,500.00 qualifies, giving him a basis of $6,611.00 for calculating his investment credit. He is therefore entitled to a credit against his taxes of $661.00.

His tax bill is thus reduced from $865.00 to $204.00. When you compare that to the $1,190.00 he would have paid without the business, you can immediately see the advantage. John's net cash advantage for the year is $2,936.00 ($1,950.00 surplus cash, plus $986.00 tax saving).

Now, before you rush out to take advantage of this apparent garden of loopholes, you should take heed of some drawbacks and disadvantages inherent in such a scheme.

In the example given, every effort was made to take advantage of as many deductions as possible **this year**. For that reason, the deductions and tax savings for future years would not be nearly as great, even though they would be there.

If you have a hobby that you would like to turn to profit, be advised that the agents of the Internal Revenue Service are not fools. They will generally permit you to try such an endeavor for a while, but they will not permit you to take tax losses indefinitely for a hobby or avocation. As a rule of thumb, if you are not turning a profit within three years, they will disallow most or many of your expense claims.

A very smart man once told me that the motel business is one of the best to get into, partly because of the investment credit mentioned above. His plan was to buy and sell motels, moving every seven or eight years (staying just long enough to make his initial investment credit stand the test of time).

He told me that after three such moves, he would be sitting pretty. He said, "The secret of this business is not the income that you receive from the rentals. The secret is in the tax saving and in the equity gain."

He got his start at the age of thirty. He inherited $20,000.00 from the estate of a rich relative, and immediately bought a small, twelve-unit motel. Now this doesn't happen very often to the average little guy but if you follow this story carefully, you will gain much insight into the uses of the invested tax credit and maybe get some investment ideas. The total price of the motel, including the land, the building, the swimming pool, and all the furniture and fixtures was $110,000.00.

The terms of the purchase were as follows: $12,000.00 down payment, with the balance of $98,000.00 to be repaid at 8% interest in 240 installments (20 years) of $800.00 each.

The average gross income from the motel was $40,000.00 per year. In the first year, my friend (we can call him Chuck) had expenses and depreciation totalling slightly more than the $40,000.00 income so he had no tax liability. Since he was unable to use his investment credit in that year, he was permitted to carry it back against previously paid taxes. YOU DO NOT LOSE THE INVESTMENT CREDIT. If you are unable to use it in the year that you make the investment, you may carry it back against taxes paid in the previous three years. If there is any unused credit after carrying it back, you may then carry it forward for the next five years. Only after that nine year period has been exhausted can you lose the investment credit.

Chuck recovered $6,000.00 by carrying back his $11,000.00 investment credit against previous taxes paid. He received a check from the government in that amount. That left him with an unused credit of $5000.00 to be carried forward against future income taxes.

Chuck kept that motel for eight years, and over that period of time, his average spendable income was $10,000.00. He paid only $2,000.00 in self-employment taxes over that period. Self Employment Tax, the equivalent of Social Security for self employed people, cannot be offset by the investment credit.

At the time of sale, Chuck's motel had increased in value considerably. He sold the motel for $140,000.00. He received $35,000.00 down payment. The new buyer took over the balance of Chuck's loan (paid down to $82,000.00), and gave Chuck a note for the $23,000.00 balance.

Since Chuck had taken depreciation on the motel at accelerated rates, his vested interest in the property at the time of sale was only $30,000.00. Since the sale price was $140,000.00, that means Chuck's gain was $110,000.00, and it qualified for long-term capital gain treatment.

Since Chuck received less than 29% of the sales price in cash, he was able to spread his gain, as an installment sale, over the twelve years of the note he received. By the way, Chuck will receive $250.00 per month income from that note.

His profit was $110,000.00 or the total $140,000.00 sale, so 79% of each dollar he received toward the principal balance was profit, and was taxed as long-term capital gains. For instance, he received $35,000.00 in the first year. Seventy-nine percent of that amount is $27,650.00. That is the amount of long-term capital gains income that must be reported in the year of sale. Since long-term capital gains are reduced by one-half before they are added to taxable income, the net tax on the sale for the year of the sale, was $2,700.00.

Now we can see how Chuck has taken $12,000.00 of his initial $20,000.00 windfall and ran it into a sizeable pot-full of money in eight years. He has increased that $12,000.00 investment to $57,000.00 ($35,000.00 down payment, plus $23,000.00 note). And all the while he had a fairly decent living income. His $10,000.00 average income was not spectacular, but when you consider that he lived in the motel as manager, it was not too shabby.

Chuck, not being the sort of fellow to rest on his laurels, immediately went shopping for another, larger mtoel. He found what he wanted very soon, a twenty-unit, deluxe motel, with a coffee shop. The price of this new motel was $220,000.00, and the owner agreed to accept $25,000.00 down payment, with the balance to be paid at $1,700.00 per month over a twenty year period.

The investment credit on the purchase price was $22,000.00. Since there were no income taxes in the previous three years, any unused credit will be carried forward to future profits. This new motel averaged a gross income of $86,000.00 per year, not including the receipts from the coffee shop.

Chuck's deductible expenses for the operation of the motel are $73,600.00, leaving him with a taxable profit of

SCHEDULE C (Form 1040)

Department of the Treasury
Internal Revenue Service

Profit or (Loss) From Business or Profession

(Sole Proprietorship)

Partnerships, Joint Ventures, etc., Must File Form 1065.

▶ Attach to Form 1040. ▶ See Instructions for Schedule C (Form 1040).

1976

Name of proprietor **CHUCK MOTELIER**

Social security number **987 65 4321**

A Principal business activity (see Schedule C Instructions) ▶ **SERVICE** ; product ▶ **MOTEL & CAFE**	
B Business name ▶ **WAGON HO MOTEL**	C Employer identification number ▶ **94-1234567**
D Business address (number and street) ▶ **12500 MAIN ST.**	
City, State and ZIP code ▶ **FRESNO, CA**	

E Indicate method of accounting: (1) ☒ Cash (2) ☐ Accrual (3) ☐ Other ▶

	Yes	No
F Were you required to file Form W-3 or Form 1096 for 1976 (see Schedule C Instructions)?	☒	
If "Yes," where filed ▶		
G Was an Employer's Quarterly Federal Tax Return, Form 941, filed for this business for any quarter in 1976?		☒

H Method of inventory valuation ▶ **FIFO** Was there any substantial change in the manner of determining quantities, costs, or valuations between the opening and closing inventories? (If "Yes," attach explanation) ☒

			Yes	No
Income	1 Gross receipts or sales $ Less: returns and allowances $ Balance ▶	1	**217,040**	
	2 Less: Cost of goods sold and/or operations (Schedule C–1, line 8)	2	**118,000**	
	3 Gross profit	3	**99,040**	
	4 Other income (attach schedule)	4		
	5 Total income (add lines 3 and 4)	5	**99,040**	
	6 Depreciation (explain in Schedule C–3)	6	**10,214**	
	7 Taxes on business and business property (explain in Schedule C–2)	7	**6,200**	
	8 Rent on business property	8	**–0–**	
	9 Repairs (explain in Schedule C–2)	9	**1,500**	
	10 Salaries and wages not included on line 3, Schedule C–1 (exclude any paid to yourself)	10	**5,000**	
	11 Insurance	11	**1,000**	
	12 Legal and professional fees	12	**2,500**	
	13 Commissions	13		
	14 Amortization (attach statement)	14		

78

Deductions

15 (a) Pension and profit-sharing plans (see Schedule C Instructions)	15(a)	
(b) Employee benefit programs (see Schedule C Instructions)	(b)	
16 Interest on business indebtedness	16	16,500 —
17 Bad debts arising from sales or services	17	
18 Depletion	18	
19 Other business expenses (specify):		
(a) SUPPLIES	5,000 —	
(b) UTILITIES	11,600 —	
(c) LINEN	2,100 —	
(d) CLEANING	4,700 —	
(e) ADVERTISING	4,000 —	
(f) PROMOTION	2,626 —	
(g) FOOD PRODUCTS	2,700 —	
(h) SMALL FURNISHINGS	1,000 —	
(i)		
(j)		
(k) Total other business expenses (add lines 19(a) through 19(j))	19(k)	31,726 00
20 Total deductions (add lines 6 through 19(k))	20	73,640 00

21 Net profit or (loss) (subtract line 20 from line 5). Enter here and on Form 1040, line 29. ALSO enter on Schedule SE, line 5(a). . . . . | 21 | 25,400 00 |

SCHEDULE C-1.—Cost of Goods Sold and/or Operations (See Schedule C Instructions for Line 2)

1 Inventory at beginning of year (if different from last year's closing inventory, attach explanation)	1	2,000 00
2 Purchases $ 55,000— Less: cost of items withdrawn for personal use $ 5,000 — Balance ▶	2	50,000 00
3 Cost of labor (do not include salary paid to yourself)	3	68,000 00
4 Materials and supplies	4	
5 Other costs (attach schedule)	5	
6 Total of lines 1 through 5	6	120,000 00
7 Less: Inventory at end of year	7	2,000 00
8 Cost of goods sold and/or operations. Enter here and on line 2 above	8	118,000 00

Did you claim a deduction for expenses of an office in your home? . . . . . ☐ Yes ☒ No

SCHEDULE C–2.—Explanation of Lines 7 and 9

Line No.	Explanation	Amount	Line No.	Explanation	Amount
7	BED TAX	$2,600—			$
7	PROPERTY TAX	3,100—			
7	PAYROLL TAX	500—			
9	APPLIANCE REPAIR	1,500—			

SCHEDULE C–3.—Depreciation (See Schedule C Instructions for Line 6)
If you need more space, use Form 4562.

a. Description of property	b. Date acquired	c. Cost or other basis	d. Depreciation allowed or allowable in prior years	e. Method of computing depreciation	f. Life or rate	g. Depreciation for this year
1 Total additional first-year depreciation (do not include in items below)						
2 Other depreciation:						
MOTEL	JAN '76	180,000—	– 0 –	S.L	40	4500 —

						Salaries and Wages
FURNITURE JAN '76	30,000	-0-	56	7	4285 -	
EQUIPMENT JAN '76	10,000	-0-	56	7	1429 -	
3 Totals	220,000			. . .	10214 -	
4 Less amount of depreciation claimed in Schedule C–1, page 1						
5 Balance—Enter here and on page 1, line 6				. . .	10214 -	

SCHEDULE C–4.—Expense Account Information (See Schedule C Instructions for Schedule C–4)

Enter information with regard to yourself and your five highest paid employees. In determining the five highest paid employees, expense account allowances must be added to their salaries and wages. However, the information need not be submitted for any employee for whom the combined amount is less than $25,000, or for yourself if your expense account allowance plus line 21, page 1, is less than $25,000.

Name	Expense account	Salaries and Wages
Owner		
1		
2		
3		
4		
5		

Did you claim a deduction for expenses connected with:
(1) Entertainment facility (boat, resort, ranch, etc.)? . . ☐ Yes ☒ No   (3) Employees' families at conventions or meetings? . . ☐ Yes ☒ No
(2) Living accommodations (except employees on business)? . ☐ Yes ☒ No   (4) Employee or family vacations not reported on Form W–2? ☐ Yes ☒ No

81

$12,400.00, coffee shop nets about $13,000.00 per year, so the combined taxable income totals $25,400.00. The self employment tax on that amount is $1,200.00.

In addition to the self employment income, Chuck also had income from his note, including $1,830.00 interest, and $1,170.00 capital gains principal. The adjusted principal was 79% of the total received, or $924.00, and the taxable portion was $462.00.

Chuck's total adjusted gross income from all sources was $27,692.00 ($25,400.00 + $1,830.00 + $462.00). The tax on that amount was $4,380.00. Since he has unused investment credit, he need only pay the self employment tax of $1,200.00. His investment credit will protect him from income taxes for the next five years.

At the end of another eight years, Chuck sold this motel and bought another one. In the eight years time, he had paid a total of $22,740.00 in taxes ($9,600.00 self employment tax, and $13,140.00 income tax for the three final, unprotected years). During this period, his annual average spendable income was in excess of $30,000.00. Chuck had to work plenty hard to earn this income, and he had very few vacation days.

On this sale, he received $50,000.00 cash down payment on a sale price of $250,000.00. As before, he carried a note for the balance of his equity in the amount of $38,000.00, payable in twelve years at $420.00 per month. Chuck's depreciated basis on the motel he sold was $140,000.00, so his profit was $110,000.00, or 44% of the sale price. That percentage was applied to the $50,000.00 he received, and so his long term capital gain for the year of sale was $22,000.00, and the tax preference effect reduced that to $11,000.00.

Chuck was now 46 years old. He had taken $12,000.00 at the age of 30, and through hard work, long hours, and taking advantage of various tax loopholes, had increased his net worth to $100,000.00. During the sixteen years, he had spendable income of $20,000.00 on the average, and had paid less than $25,000.00 in taxes through the years. What's more, almost half of the taxes he paid were Self

Employment Tax, and as such, are available for him to draw at age 62.

But Chuck didn't want to wait until age 62 to retire. He found another motel similar to the one he had just sold. The purchase price of the new motel and coffee shop was also $250,000.00. Chuck made a down payment of $50,000.00, with terms of $1,750.00 per month for twenty years.

The income and expenses for the new place were almost exactly the same as for the old one. For the next five years, Chuck paid only his self employment tax, while his investment credit absorbed his income tax.

Chuck is now 51 years old. He has hired a manager to run the motel for him. He has managed to save some of his $30,000.00+ annual income from the past thirteen years. After paying the manager a substantial salary, Chuck still has $12,000.00 per year from the business. In addition to that, he also has $420.00 per month coming from the last note (the first note was paid off one year ago), and those payments will come in for another seven years. He also has some interest from his savings.

At age 51, Chuck has achieved the American Dream. He has virtually retired, with an annual income of $18,000.00. He has substantial equity in a profitable investment property. Through the benefit of legal tax loopholes and benefits, he has accomplished this without paying a large tax burden. His total tax bill for the twenty-one years that it took him to get where he is totals only $35,000.00, more than half of which is self employment tax.

Now, the ever present word of warning. There is no guarantee that the investment credit will always be with us. In fact, it is scheduled to be reduced from 10% to 7% in 1977. And there is no way we can be absolutely certain that the capital gains loophole will not be rescinded.

Also, we realize that these figures are somewhat grand, and might seem over the head of the little guy. But they do show an accurate example of what can be done.

FARMING

Don't feel too sorry for the poor farmers. They might get the short end of the stick sometimes, but they have a multitude of tax loopholes that the rest of us cannot take advantage of.

Special tax rules give farmers tax breaks that are not generally available to other businessmen. These rules apply to accounting and inventory methods, capital gain treatment in some cases, and the deduction of items that are normally capital expenses. These benefits extend to sideline farmers, and also to investors.

Farmers have accounting options that include the cash method, the accrual method, and with consent of the IRS, the crop method. For tax purposes, the cash method in generally preferable to the accrual method. This is because the increase in value of produce or livestock during the year is not taxable under the cash method but is taxable under the accrual method.

As an illustration, during a farm's first year of operation, it had $3,000.00 of expenses, $8,000.00 of income, and at the end of the year, it had livestock worth $2,000.00. Under the cash method, the taxable income was $5,000.00 Under the accrual method the taxable income was $7,000.00, because the inventoried livestock were considered as income in that year.

Sometimes the accrual method can be an advantage, especially in tax planning. For instance, if a farmer sells some grain in December, but is not paid until the following January, under the cash method, his income would be reported in the new year, while his expense (planting, seed, fertilizer, etc.) was incurred in the prior year. Under the accrual system, the income would be reported in the same year as the sale, regardless of when he actually receives the money.

A farmer may use the crop method of reporting income from crops for which the process of planting, harvesting and sale is not completed within the same taxable year. This could be a total period of less than 12 months, spanning two tax years. This method may be elected only with the express consent of the IRS, regardless of when the taxpayer seeks to make it.

Under the crop method, all expenses of the crop, including the expenses of seed or young plants, are charged to the crop and all receipts are credited to the crop. The profit or loss is realized and included in income only in the year the crop is harvested and sold.

These different accounting methods are not to be taken lightly. You cannot jump back and forth from one method to another just for your own convenience. In order to change accounting methods, you must obtain permission from the Internal Revenue Service in advance.

Some farm products are eligible for preferential tax treatment. Gain and loss on an unharvested crop that is sold along with the underlying land qualifies for special treatment. If there is a loss, it is considered an ordinary loss. If there is a gain, it is considered a capital gain, if the following tests are met:

1. The land was used in the business;
2. The land was held for more than six months;
3. And the crop and land are sold at the same time, and in the same transaction.

Certain livestock also qualifies for this capital gain/ordinary loss treatment. If the livestock is held for sale to customers as inventory, the gain is ordinary income. But if the livestock is held for work, breeding, dairy, or sporting purposes, the sale comes under the capital gain/ordinary loss rule, provided the animals are held for specified minimum holding periods.

Those periods are:

Cattle and horses, must be held for twenty-four months from the date of purchase, they must have been held for one of the purposes listed above for that time, and all other livestock must be held for twelve months from the date of purchase, and also must meet all the other requirements.

Such animals also qualify for depreciation. The purchase of a bull for breeding purposes is a capital investment. You should spread the cost over the

SCHEDULE F (Form 1040)

Department of the Treasury
Internal Revenue Service

Farm Income and Expenses

(Compute social security self-employment tax on Schedule SE)

► Attach to Form 1040 or Form 1065. ► See Instructions for Schedule F (Form 1040).
► If rental income, see instructions before using this schedule.

1976

Name of proprietor(s) _HIRAM H. HOWELL_

Business name and address _TRIPLE H RANCH_

Location of farm(s) and number of acres in each farm _KANSAS - 100 ACRES_

Social security number _876:54:3210_

Employer identification number (See instructions) _____

Part I — Farm Income—Cash Receipts and Disbursements Method

Do not include sales of livestock held for draft, breeding, sport, or dairy purposes; report such sales on Form 4797.

Sales of Purchased Livestock and Other Items Purchased for Resale

a. Description	b. Amount received	c. Cost or other basis
1 Livestock:	$ 12,000 —	$ 3,000 —
2 Other Items:		
3 Totals	$ 12,000 —	$ 3,000 —
4 Profit or (loss), subtract line 3, column c from line 3, column b . . . . . ▲	$ 9,000 —	

Sales of Market Livestock and Produce Raised and Held Primarily for Sale and Other Farm Income

Kind	Quantity	Amount
5 Cattle	20	$ 6,200 —
6 Calves		
7 Sheep		
8 Swine		

Part II — Farm Deductions—For Cash and Accrual Method Taxpayers

Do not include personal or living expenses not attributable to production of farm income, such as taxes, insurance, repairs, etc., on your dwelling.

Items	Amount
29 Labor hired	$ 1,200 —
30 Repairs, maintenance .	2,350 —
31 Interest	1,700 —
32 Rent of farm, pasture	
33 Feed purchased . .	6,100 —
34 Seeds, plants purchased	
35 Fertilizers, lime, chemicals	
36 Machine hire . .	
37 Supplies purchased .	450 —
38 Breeding fees . .	
39 Veterinary fees, medicine	400 —
40 Gasoline, fuel, oil .	
41 Storage, warehousing	
42 Taxes	600 —

86

9 Poultry · · · · ·		
10 Dairy products · ·		
11 Eggs · · · ·		
12 Wool · · ·		
13 Cotton · · ·		
14 Tobacco · · ·		
15 Vegetables · ·		
16 Grain · · · ·		
17 Fruits and nuts · ·		
18 Other (specify): ⋯⋯⋯		

OTHER FARM INCOME

19 Machine work · · · · ·		
20 (a) Patronage dividends (See Sch. F instructions) · ·		
(b) Per-unit retains (See Sch. F instructions) · ·		
21 Nonpatronage distributions from exempt cooperatives ·		
22 Agricultural program payments:		
(a) Cash · · · ·		
(b) Materials and services · ·		
23 Commodity credit loans under election (or forfeited) · ·		
24 Federal gasoline tax credit · · ·		
25 State gasoline tax refund · · ·		
26 Other (specify): ⋯⋯⋯		
27 Add lines 5 through 26 · · · · · ▲	$ 6,200	–
28 Gross profits *(add lines 4 and 27) · · · · ▲	$ 15,200	–

54 Net farm profit or (loss) (subtract line 53 from 28). Enter here and on Form 1040, line 33 or on Form 1065, line 9. ALSO enter on Schedule SE, Part I, line 1(a) · · · · ▲

* Use amount on line 28 for optional method of computing net earnings from self-employment. (See Schedule SE, Part I, line 3.)

43 Insurance · · · · ·		
44 Utilities · · · ·		
45 Freight, trucking · ·		
46 Conservation expenses · ·		
47 Land clearing expenses · ·		
48 Pension and profit-sharing plans (see Sch. F instructions) · ·		
49 Employee benefit programs other than line 48 (see Sch. F instructions) · ·		
50 Other (specify): ⋯⋯⋯		
51 Add lines 29 through 50 ▲	$	
52 Depreciation (from line 57, Part III) · · · ·	3,300	–
53 Total deductions. Add lines 51 and 52 · · · · ▲	$ 15,100	–

$ ⟨ 100 00 ⟩

87

reasonable and useful life of the animal, instead of claiming it in the year of purchase.

A farm, unlike most businesses, can lose money for long periods of time. It is not unprecedented for a farm to lose money for ten consecutive years without losing its tax status. The main thing you must prove is that you are attempting to make a profit. However, if you are not a full time farmer, you should be prepared to have the IRS consider your farming as a hobby if you have not shown a profit in two of the past five years (or two out of seven for breeding, training, showing or racing horses).

Our example this time is Hiram Howell, owner of the Triple H cattle ranch in central Kansas. Hiram's ranch is 100 acres, completely fenced and irrigated, with a ranch house, a large barn, and several outbuildings.

He is a cash method farmer, and raises some of his own stock, while also buying and selling cattle. This past year, Hiram sold 50 head of cattle, some of which were purchased for resale, and others he had raised on the ranch. He also sold six breeding cows, and one bull. All of the breeding animals had been held for the required twenty-four months in a breeding capacity, and were eligible for capital gain treatment.

Of the first fifty sold, thirty had been purchased for resale. The net income from the sale of these animals was $9,000.00. The twenty that had been born and raised on the ranch brought in $6,200.00.

The six breeding cows had been purchased at a cost of $2,400.00 and had been depreciated over the past three years to a value of $1,200.00. Hiram sold these six for $1,800.00, realizing a gain of $600.00 ($1,800.00 minus $1,200.00 current value). The bull had been purchased for $1,500.00 five years ago, and had been depreciated down to $300.00. The sale price of the bull was $400.00, leaving a gain of $100.00.

Hiram's expenses in running the farm included depreciation of his barn and outbuildings, farm equipment, transportation equipment, and remaining breeding animals. Other expenses were for labor, repairs, interest, feed, supplies, veterinary fees, fuel, taxes, insurance, utilities, brand inspection, and so forth.

Hiram's expenses, including depreciation totalled $15,100.00. His ordinary income came to $15,200.00, and his taxable income from long term capital gains was $350.00, making an adjusted gross income of $450.00.

His actual cash position was somewhat better than his taxable situation. He actually received $15,200.00, plus $2,200.00, for a total income of $17,400.00, while his actual cash expenses were only $11,800.00 (the remainder being depreciation), for a net cash gain of $5,600.00. When you consider that he was permitted to eat the meat he raised without paying income tax on his own consumption, he didn't do too badly.

Chapter 8

Losses

Profits and losses, bad debts, etc. If you must sustain a loss, how to minimize the financial hurt of that loss. How to take advantage of the loopholes and use them to offset business setbacks. An example of how a small businessman used Net Operating Loss Carryback to save his business. Bad debts are deductible. The difference between business bad debts and personal ones. What about partially worthless debts? Which debts qualify?

For the purposes of definition, we are going to talk about two different types of losses in this chapter. The first type is the opposite of profit . . . when you lose money in business. The second type is when you have a bad debt.

Naturally enough, nobody wants to lose money. However, for a short time, a well capitalized business can lose money without suffering too badly. In fact, there are tax loopholes designed to assist the businessman in this position.

Bill Scott is the owner of Scotty's Shell Service, a thriving gasoline and service station located on a major highway and right in the middle of the town where he lives. Scotty has been in business for ten years in the same location, and has built up a decent local trade. But it has not always been so. When he first started, Scotty catered to the highway traffic. He was happy with the high volume of gasoline he pumped, and did not work hard to develop the service business from local citizens. He was satisfied to leave that part of the business to the other station operators. He was making plenty just on the gasoline sales.

Then, one summer, the highway department decided to make extensive repairs to that section of the highway. They decided to resurface the roadway completely, taking the old pavement out, grading, filling in a new bed, and then paving. Scotty knew that his business would suffer in the short run because of the resulting difficulty of access to the station, but he figured he could stay open, sell a few gallons, and make a little money. Also, he figured, it would only inconvenience him for a couple of weeks. And even though it was in his peak summer season, he figured the long run gains would compensate for the short run losses.

What he didn't figure was the weather. Right in the middle of the project, and right when an automobile would have to scale an eight-inch curb to get from the highway into the station, it rained; an unseasonable downpour that lasted for a week, and delayed progress on the highway work for an additional two weeks.

Two days after the highway crews started back on the job, the local union called a strike. This put the highway project another ten days behind schedule. All during this time, Scotty's Shell Service sat virtually isolated and free of income-producing traffic. The net result was that Scotty had very little income for a period of eight weeks, right in the middle of his peak earning season.

Well, Scotty started figuring again. During the last five years he had done pretty well. He had made an average of $14,000.00 per year, and had been wise enough to save some rainy day money. This savings pulled him through

Form 1045
(Rev. Feb. 1974)
Department of the Treasury
Internal Revenue Service

Application for Tentative Refund
(From Carryback of Net Operating Loss, Unused Investment Credit, or Unused Work
Incentive (WIN) Program Credit)
▶ For use by taxpayers other than corporations.

Do Not Attach to Your
Income Tax Return—
File Separately to
Expedite Processing

Please type or print

Name

WILLIAM SCOTT

Number and street

110 COOPER AVE.

City or town, State and ZIP code

PROVO, UTAH

Employer identification number

N/A

Your social security number

876-54-3210

Spouse's social security number

1 Return for year of net operating loss, unused investment credit, and unused WIN credit

(a) Tax year ended ▶ 12-31-74

(b) Date filed ▶ 4-15-75

(c) Service center where filed SALT LAKE CITY

2 This application is filed to carryback ▶

(a) Net operating loss Amount $3,600.00

(b) Unused investment credit Amount $

(c) Unused WIN credit Amount $

3 (a) Preceding tax year(s) affected by carryback

(b) Did spouse file a separate return

3d ☐ Yes ☒ No
2d ☐ Yes ☒ No
1st ☐ Yes ☒ No

(c) Service center or office where return(s) filed (City and State)

(d) Amount of unpaid income tax

(e) Amount of other unpaid taxes (specify)

4 If you changed your accounting period, give date permission to change was granted ▶

5 Have you filed a petition in Tax Court for the year or years to which the carryback is to be applied? . . . ☐ Yes ☒ No

Computation of Decrease in Tax	3d preceding tax year ended ▶ 1971		2d preceding tax year ended ▶ 1972		1st preceding tax year ended ▶ 1973	
	(a) As last determined	(b) After carryback	(c) As last determined	(d) After carryback	(e) As last determined	(f) After carryback
6 Adjusted gross income before adjustment for carryback . . .	14,200-	14,200-	14,400-	14,400-	280-	280-
7 Net operating loss deduction resulting from carryback . . .		3,600-		-0-		-0-
8 Line 6 less line 7 . . . Note: Individuals who use tax table, skip to line 13, enter the tax. Otherwise, go to line 9.	14,200-	10,600-	14,400-	14,400-	280-	280-

Line	Description					
9	Total of itemized deductions; or the standard deduction	2,420 -				
10	Line 8 less line 9	11,780 -	2,420 -			
11	Exemptions	1,500 -	8,180 -			
12	Taxable income, line 10 less 11 .	10,280 -	1,500 -	1,500 -		6,680 -
13	Income tax liability (see instruction J)	1,882 -	1,129 -	1,905 -	1,908 -	-0-
14	Foreign tax credit (disregard if tax table or standard deduction is used)					
15	Retirement income credit . . .					
16	Investment credit (see instruction H)					
17	WIN credit (see instruction I) .					
18	Total credits on lines 14 through 17					
19	Line 13 less line 18	1,882 -	1,129 -	1,905 -	1,908 -	-0-
20	Tax from recomputing prior year investment credit					
21	Tax from recomputing prior year WIN credit					
22	Minimum tax (see instruction J) .					
23	Total tax liability (add lines 19, 20, 21, and 22)	1,882 -	1,129 -	1,908 -	1,908 -	-0-
24	Enter amounts from line 23, columns (b), (d), and (f) . . .	1,129 -	1,905 -		-0-	-0-
25	Decrease in tax (line 23 less 24) .	753.00	-0-		-0-	-0-

Under penalties of perjury, I declare that I have examined this application (including any accompanying schedules and statements), and to the best of my knowledge and belief it is true, correct, and complete.

(Applicant's signature and date)

(If application is filed jointly by husband and wife both must sign)

(Wife's signature and date)

93

that year, because the net from his business was almost exactly break-even.

Things will be better next year, Scotty figured. With the highway all fixed up, more and more people will travel through this town, and I can't help but do better, he figured.

Once again, something unexpected interfered with Scotty's figuring. The "energy crisis" came along, forcing the prices of gasoline to double in a few short months. All service stations were given limited allocations of gasoline. Those allocations were based on the amount of gasoline pumped the previous year. And due to the unusual highway situation, Scotty had not pumped anywhere near what he would have normally.

So Scotty was left with short rations. He had no trouble selling all the gasoline he could get. People lined up for blocks to buy his gasoline. But the amount of gasoline he could get was small. And to top it off, even when the allocations eased, the traffic that normally poured down the highway was reduced to a trickle. The government's campaign to make people conscious of fuel conservation was successful, and they were not driving nearly as much.

So Scotty had another disastrous year, even worse than the previous one. The net loss of the business for the year was $3,600.00. However, Scotty was able to recover part of that loss through a tax loophole known as the Net Operating Loss Carryback.

As with the Investment Credit Carryback, the N.O.L. Carryback goes back three years for its recovery. Since Scotty was in a 22% tax bracket in the carryback year, he recovered that percentage of his loss, or $753.00.

Bad debts differ from other deductible items in certain respects: They are deductible even though not connected with business or income producing activities; A partial deduction may be allowed if the debt is only partially worthless; In some cases, a bad debt deduction is allowed for additions to a bad debt reserve, thus permitting a deduction for an anticipated bad debt loss; Individuals may deduct bad debts whether or not they itemize their deductions; The statute of limitations is extended for refund claims on bad debts.

Bad debts that are owed to a taxpayer other than a corporation may be either business or nonbusiness. The rules for deducting business bad debts are more liberal than for deducting nonbusiness bad debts.

A debt is defined as a valid, enforceable obligation arising from a debtor-creditor relationship. There must be an obligation to pay a fixed or easy-to-determine sum of money. Additionally, there **should** be a reasonable chance for repayment, although this is not necessarily an absolute requirement.

The distinction between business and non-business bad debts is important because business bad debts have the following advantages over non-business:

1. Business bad debts are completely deductible against income. Non-business bad debts are short term capital losses, and as such they come under the capital loss limitations. For 1976, that limitation is $1,000.00. In 1977, the amount of capital loss that can be claimed in any one year increased to $2,000.00, and in 1978 and thereafter, the amount increases to $3,000.00.

2. Business debts qualify for deduction under the bad debts reserve method, while non-business debts do not. The reserve method for deducting business bad debts means that you may deduct an expense based on the loss that you reasonably anticipate from experience.

3. Business debts are deductible when they are only partly worthless.

To differentiate between business debts and non-business debts we should remember the following rules of a business debt: A business debt is either a debt created or acquired in the course of your trade or business, or a debt that is related to your business at the time it becomes worthless. Any other loss **at all** is non-business.

If you loan your brother-in-law $5,000.00 to go into business, that is a non-business debt. The only exception would be if you were actively in the business of lending money. If your brother-in-law fails in his business and is unable to repay the loan, you are entitled to claim a non-business bad debt loss. You must complete Schedule D, in the section on Assets Held Not More Than Six Months, showing the date of the loan, the date you wrote it off, and the amount of the loss. The amount of the loss that you can claim is subject to the limitations under #1 above.

If on the other hand, you invest $5,000.00 in the brother-in-law's business, you do not have a bad debt loss at all. A capital contribution is not a debt. The deciding factor of whether an investment is a loan or a capital contribution is the repayment consideration. If repayment is not tied to the success of the venture, chances are you have a loan.

While we are on the subject of brothers-in-laws, or any other relative for that matter, words of caution are important. Courts and Internal Revenue Service auditors closely scrutinize transactions between related people to see if their is a valid debtor-creditor relationship.

Loans to relatives can be valid debts, but be certain that you treat the loan in a businesslike manner, with a note indicating the amount and the date and method of repayment. Otherwise, you might as well consider the loan as a gift, and be happy when you get repaid. You will have considerable difficulty convincing an IRS auditor that you are entitled to a bad debt loss.

Business bad debt losses are normally of two types. By far the most common is the case of a merchant who sells his wares on credit. He normally counts the sale as profit at the time of the sale, and enters the amount owed as an account receivable on his ledger. He pays sales tax, if any, at the time of the sale, and it is reported as income. If the debt becomes worthless at some time after the end of his tax year, the merchant can claim the loss as a bad debt. He can do this since he has already claimed the entire sale as income.

On the same token, if the merchant receives a check for payment of a debt, and the check is dishonored by the bank, he can claim a bad debt loss, providing it happens over the year end as mentioned above.

Another, less common, type of business debt occurs when a taxpayer makes a loan to a customer, client, supplier, or other business-related person. Should such a loan become worthless, it would be considered a business bad debt.

One important thing to remember, before you can declare a debt to be worthless, you must make strenuous efforts to collect. For example, you make a loan to an individual who later declares bankruptcy. On the surface, it would appear that your loan is worthless, but Internal Revenue Service might decide that you should have made efforts after the bankruptcy to collect the loan. Such a failure on your part to make an attempt might prompt an IRS auditor to disallow your deduction. That does not mean it is gone forever, but it does mean that you must make further attempts to collect the debt before you can write it off.

As with other deductions mentioned in this book, never let lack of absolute proof stop you from making a legitimate claim. If you make a loan, without putting it in writing, and it later becomes worthless, you should claim the deduction. Sure, if you are audited you will need proof, but let Internal Revenue Service disallow the deduction. Don't take it on yourself to disallow any genuine deductible expense.

Chapter 9

An IRS Audit (Heaven Forbid!)

What happens when you are chosen for an audit. How to act at an audit. What to bring with you. Seeking professional help. Records, their importance, and how they should be kept. What are your chances in being chosen for audit. Internal audits vs. field audits. Being prepared to answer possible questions. How to beat the fear/intimidation tactics of the IRS. Preparing for a field audit and requesting a delay. Using the courts. If you're convinced you're right don't be afraid of court.

Repeatedly throughout this book, you have been advised that the only time receipts are really important are if and when the Internal Revenue Service selects your tax return for an audit. This is it, baby! If they call you, or notify you in any way that your return is going to be audited, you had better dig through all the old files, rummage through the attic, call the bank for interest verification, and look everywhere for those receipts. Remember, we said receipts were not necessary for you to claim a deduction. WE DID NOT SAY THAT YOU WOULD NEVER NEED THEM.

The first thing to keep in mind is that the better your records are, the better you are going to fare in an audit. If you are the sort of person that keeps accurate, detailed records of all income and expense items, then the auditor is going to love you. The reason for this response is that many taxpayers do not keep such records. In fact, the shoe box method of bookkeeping is probably much more common than entries on a ledger.

You should be advised that just because the auditor admires your bookkeeping records, you should not expect the auditor to take it easy on you. What it amounts to is that you are making his job easier. And there is a psychological advantage to be gained there. The auditor is much more likely to take your word for something if your records are in order. When you use the shoe box method, you will often end up asking the auditor to take your word for **many** entries.

Records or no records, the first thing you should do if you are audited is to call in professional assistance. We will benefit financially from your call. In this audit situation, you will be facing an expert in the tax law. You need all the help you can get.

Are you scared so far? Don't be ashamed to admit it. Remember the old intimidation that the Internal Revenue Service (and all phases of government, for that matter) holds over us. The trick is the same as when handling animals . . . don't let them know that you are afraid. IRS agents, like animals, can sense fear. They are exposed to similar situations every day of the week. Their intuition is so ingrained by experience that they instinctively know if you are frightened.

The chances are pretty good that you are a first-timer, though. The plain fact is that less than one tax return in twenty, that is less than 5% of all the tax returns filed, is audited. And if you are a little guy, your percentage goes down even more. The actual statistics are not made public, but it is estimated that less than two percent (1 in 50) of wage earners under the $20,000.00 income level are audited. Or another way of looking at it, if you are audited once in fifty years, you will be just about average for that income level.

There are two different types of Internal Revenue Service audits. By their own terminology, they are called "Internal Audits" and "Field Audits." Both audits look at the same information, but from different stances.

The internal audit arises from one or more irregular entries on your tax return. The Internal Revenue Service will write you, and frequently telephone you, to make an appointment for you to come into their nearest office for the audit. For the most part, this audit meeting is set at your convenience, with the exception that government employees do not work on weekends.

And therein lies one of the inequities of the system. The IRS agent is on salary. He is being paid for the time he spends with you. You, on the other hand, are sacrificing at least one day's income. Your expenses connected with an audit are deductible, but you cannot claim a deduction for your loss of income.

You should take your tax return, along with your receipts, into an accountant or qualified tax practitioner. That expert should be able to review your records and reasonably predict the problem areas, if any. Whether he accompanies you to the Internal Revenue office is a matter of choice to you. The main thing is that you should be prepared.

That is the key word . . . PREPARED. The auditor will most certainly be prepared, and in order to get equal footing, you must do your homework.

It cannot be overemphasized . . . to get past the intimidation of an IRS auditor, you must get over your fear. The best way to overcome that fear is to arm yourself with facts. If you are still uncertain or uneasy, retain a tax expert to represent you, or accompany you to the audit.

Normally, when called in for an office audit, the taxpayer will be facing an auditor of limited experience. This is due to the need of the Internal Revenue Service to assign their best agents to bigger fish. Sometimes this relative inexperience can work in your advantage, but more often it is the other way around.

The office auditor is frequently new on the job, and is consequently underpaid. He is anxious to prove that he can do a good job and is qualified for promotion. And whether IRS admits it or not, these beginning auditors are graded as much on the revenue they produce as on the quality of the work they do.

If you have prepared carefully, you can sometimes turn the intimidation around. It is a certainty that you know much more about your individual situation than the auditor can possibly know. And if you do your homework, you probably know more about your taxes than he does. Hold your ground when you know that you are right. On questionable matters, and there are many tax matters that are not clear cut, the best approach is to present your side of the argument logically and firmly.

There is little or nothing to be gained by taking an aggressive or angry stance. The auditor has nothing against you personally. He is just trying to do his job **as he sees it**. What you must accomplish is to make him see your individual tax problem from your point of view.

On the other hand, don't waste your time trying to make friends with the auditor. Your only concern should be to persuade him that you are correct in your claims, and that he can put his time to better use on someone else's tax return. In other words, try to make his basic goal (pleasing his boss) work to your advantage.

Another normal feature of an office audit is that it will ordinarily cover only one year's tax return. They might ask you to bring in prior tax returns, but they do not usually audit those. The reason that they want the previous year's return is to examine it for significant variations, and to compare such ongoing things as depreciation.

A field audit is a horse of a different color. The auditor that you will encounter in a field audit is very likely a pro. He will know his stuff, and will have been exposed to every imaginable trick. The same rule that applied to an office audit goes double here. BE PREPARED!

A field audit will frequently be for more than the current year. Two years' and sometimes three years' returns will be reviewed. This makes your job of preparation much more difficult.

Because of the difficulty of this preparation, you can ordinarily get a delay for a field audit. These auditors have been known to telephone your home, or even knock on your door, asking for an immediate audit. It is not usually in your best interest to allow them entry for an audit under such circumstances. You had better believe that they will be prepared, so you should ask for a delay to make certain that you are equally well prepared to defend yourself.

An Internal Revenue Service agent once informed me that a field audit was normally called for if fraud was suspected. I do not believe that is always the case. In one circumstance that comes to mind, many individuals were selected for field audits because they had gone to a particular tax practitioner for their tax preparation. This practitioner was a well-qualified man, formerly an IRS agent, who had earned a reputation in Internal Revenue Service circles for stretching the truth and preparing falsified tax returns.

Whether that tax practitioner was guilty or not, he did not personally suffer the wrath of IRS. Instead, the individual taxpayers, his customers, were subjected to field audits. In some cases, they had to pay more taxes, and other cases they did not. But in all cases, they were caught relatively unaware and unprepared to defend their deductions. In all cases, they were forced to endure the fear and dread of a TAX AUDIT.

Your preparation for a field audit will likely be more difficult, due to the multiple year aspect. For that reason, if and when the auditor calls, you should ask for at least a two week delay to get ready. And more time would naturally be better.

How do you handle this auditor? As was mentioned, this person is a professional. He has seen all the tricks. He has been charmed and he has been threatened. He has learned to see through the efforts of people to distract him from his task. Don't spend your energy trying to get him off the track. Remember, he is on the payroll during the entire time. He has all day, but you are not being paid for your time.

Once again, be prepared. Have your tax consultant review the return, along with your receipts, for possible problems. If you can anticipate his questions, you have a much better chance of answering them.

Supposing you and the auditor have a major difference of opinion concerning the deductibility of an expense. If you have prepared yourself to defend this expense, and you are still unable to convince the auditor, what can you do? You can ask for a conference with his supervisor.

Surprisingly, very few taxpayers take this step. It is surprising because it is so simple, and it is often effective. Especially in the case of an office audit, where the supervisor is available, this procedure is most helpful. In a very high percentage of cases that are referred to the supervisor for an informal review, there is some concession made. But don't waste your time and their time by debating lost causes or small issues.

If the auditor decides against you, and your conference with the supervisor is unsuccessful, and you remain certain that your interpretation is correct, you still have the recourse of the courts.

If you hesitate to appeal because you think you can't win, think again. Of those who take their cases to the U.S. Tax Court, about 10% win. Another 30% get compromises. The higher courts have even more favorable statistics—20% of the cases end in decisions where the taxpayer wins. By all means, appeal.

The first step is the district conference. This is a part of the administrative appeals process within the IRS itself. Here officials called district conferees can weigh individual cases and decide whether the IRS should stick to its original decision or settle the case with a compromise.

If the tax law itself is questioned, you may take your case to the Appelate Conference. This is the highest level of appeals within the IRS administrative system. However, most people bypass this level and go directly to the court system.

If you think you can prove that you are being charged more tax than you owe, you should go to the U.S. Tax Court. Just remember—**you** must prove the IRS wrong; they don't have to establish proof to show that their audit is correct.

There is also a small case division of this court. If the amount in question is $1500 or less, this is generally an easier way to go in hopes of a favorable decision.

If you think the IRS owes you a refund and choose not to go to the tax court, you may go to the U.S. District Court. Although the burden of proof is still on the taxpayer, the IRS has become a defendent in a suit. They owe you money.

With the same jurisdictions and powers is the U.S. Court of Claims. This Court is held only in Washington, D.C., the same city in which the IRS is located. From here and also from the U.S. District Courts, you can go directly to the Supreme Court.

Glossary

Adjusted Gross Income—A taxpayer's income before taking any exemptions or deductions. This is **not** total income, but reflects deductions of non-taxable income such as: social security benefits, one half of long term capital gains, business expenses, etc.

Audit—The process of official IRS review of an individual's or corporation's tax returns. This usually requires a personal appearance before the IRS auditor with all available records of the year in question.

Average Gross Income—An average of the taxpayer's gross income (see adjusted gross income) over a given number of years.

Basis—The word "basis," for income tax purposes, is used mainly in determining the amount of gain or loss on the sale of property, or in computing depreciation. It represents what the property cost, but it is adjusted by other influences, such as improvements in the case of sale, or salvage value in the case of depreciation.

"Bounty Hunters"—In these times taken to mean those people who anonymously inform the IRS that they suspect another person of filing an incorrect tax return. These people can receive a "bounty" of 1% to 10% of any money collected by the IRS resulting from such a tip. (See Chapter 1 for the history of these "bounty hunters.")

Capital Improvements—Those improvements to a taxpayer's home or business that have required an expenditure of money during the stated business year. The expense of capital improvements must be spread over a period of years through depreciation.

Capital Investments—Direct investments of monies by the taxpayer: such as stocks, bonds, real estate, mortgages, etc.

Carrybacks And Carryovers—There are three types of carrybacks—the Net Operating Loss Carryback, the Capital Loss Carryover, and the Investment Credit Carryback. With the NOL and Investment Credit carrybacks, the procedure is the same. First you may carryback three years, to the earliest year. Then work forward through the next two years. If there is any NOL or credit remaining, it may be carried forward for seven years. The Capital Loss Carryover, for individuals, can be carried indefinitely.

Casualty Loss—A one-time, sudden loss sustained by the taxpayer: such as destruction by fire or wind, theft, or other disaster. Not meant to include any loss sustained over a period of time or on a gradual basis.

Charities—Any legally constituted non-profit organization so designated by the state and federal governments as being able to accept contributions of monies or materials.

Contributions—Any monies or materials given or donated to a recognized charity. (See charities.)

Declining Balance Method—A method for computing depreciation using the year-end balance subtracted from balance at the beginning of the tax year. This method gives a more accurate picture of the accelerated reduction of value during the first few years of an assets use. (See also depreciation.)

Dependent—One who receives a major share (usually over 50%) of his or her financial support from the taxpayer for the tax year, and who's support entitles the taxpayer to deduct a dependancy allowance from his/her taxes for that year.

Depletion—A tax deduction that may be taken by a taxpayer owning a non-renewable resource such as minerals or oil wells.

Depreciation—The allowance for the declining value of a physical property or tangible asset owned by the taxpayer. More specifically: the yearly reduction in value of such things as tools, motor vehicles, machinery, etc. (For computation of depreciation see also declining balance method and straight line method.)

Disallow—The term used by the IRS to indicate their disapproval of a deduction or method used by the taxpayer in the computation of his/her taxes.

Dividend—That part of a company's monies set aside for dispersal to shareholders in that company. This is usually done by the company with profits figured after they have paid their taxes, but some companies pay dividends out of a general fund; thus avoiding what is in effect "double taxation." (See: double taxation.)

Double Taxation—Refers to the fact that people often are taxed twice on the same income. For example, dividends are usually paid from a company's profits after they have been taxed; these dividends are also considered taxable income by those receiving them, and must be included in income tax computations by the taxpayer.

Equity—The current cash value, actually owned and paid

for already, of an asset. For example: a machine purchased at $20,000.00 plus interest over a five year period; total price $24,000.00. At the end of three years the purchaser's equity in the machine would be approximately $12,000.00 if the value of the machine remained the same.

Exclusion—The portion of a taxpayer's income that is not included in the computation of his/her taxes. For example: veteran's benefits, interest on certain bonds, social security benefits, etc.

Exemption—Allowances made to the taxpayer enabling him/her to deduct members of the household, (standard exemptions: self, spouse, dependant children and relatives) for whom he/she is the major source of support. Also used to denote certain tax-exempt contributions and/or earnings.

Fringe Benefits—Those payments to employees of a noncash nature. Not salary. These may be in the form of health insurance, life insurance, stock options, expense accounts, and many others.

Gift Tax—A tax levied on the taxpayer when he transfers over certain amounts of property in his/her lifetime. The allowed amount per year is $3000.00 ($6000.00 for husband and wife filing jointly) with an additional $30,000.00 ($60,000.00 for husband and wife filing jointly) during one's lifetime.

Income Averaging—A method for eliminating large "highs" and "lows" in income. Especially useful for persons receiving large amounts of money one year and much lower amounts over preceeding or succeeding years. For example: An author who's yearly salary fluctuates by more than one-third over a five year period. This large yearly salary may be averaged with the other four yearly salaries and one-fifth of that total paid for each one of the five years.

Interest—The percentage charged or paid to loan or borrow monies over a set period of time. (For methods of computing interest see straight line method and sum-of-the-digits-method.)

Investment Tax Credit—A credit against a liability for income tax that is based on the purchase of a tangible depreciable asset with a useful life of three years or more. The basis for the credit depends on the useful life of the asset: 100% of cost for 7 years or more; 66 2/3% of cost for 5—6 years; 33 1/3% of cost for 3—4 years; nothing on 1—2 years. The credit is 10% of the basis.

IRA—Individual Retirement Account. An account that follows the provisions of the Keogh Plan whereby an individual can deposit a limited amount, (see: Keogh Plan,) with a bank. The bank acting as trustee administers this account which serves as a personal retirement plan.

Itemized Deductions—The separate listing of all expenses to be taken off one's taxes. This is usually done when one or more of these expenses exceeds the standard deduction allowed by the IRS, and can substantially reduce the amount owed.

Keogh Plan—A government plan enabling a taxpayer to virtually set up his own retirement plan. This plan allows you to deposit 15% of your gross income, (up to $7,500.00 for the self employed) with a bank in a special account. The bank acts as trustee and may invest this money in common stock, bank savings, government notes, and a few similar type investments.

Long Term Capital Gains—Profits made on the sale or exchange of property and/or assets held more than six months and are not normally used in association with the taxpayer's normal line of business. The Tax Reform Act of 1976 will change the time period to nine months in 1977 and to one year in 1978. These profits are taxed at a maximum rate of 50% of capital gains included with taxable income. That means that in no case can the tax on long term capital gains be more than half the tax-rate on regular income.

Personal Property—A tax for other than income and real estate. Vehicle registration and use taxes are personal property type taxes. The tax definition clearly defines personal property as movable rather than fixed property as in the case of real estate.

Points—Many real estate sale include points. Points are usually charged by the seller as a kind of bonus to be paid by the buyer to the seller. Each point is one percent of the total sale price. Thus, if a house sells for $42,500 and the seller requires a 15% down payment and three points, one must pay $6,375 for the down payment plus $1,275 for the points (3% of $42,500.)

Prepayment Penalty—A charge imposed by the lending institution when the borrower pays off a loan before it is due. The interest due must be rebated to the borrower, but the lender is allowed to charge a smaller fee as a partial compensation for the loss of revenue.

Promotional Entertainment—That entertainment directly concerned with improving or promoting the taxpayer's business interests. This does not mean that the taxpayer may take his wife to dinner, tell her to talk about the business for 30 seconds, and then deduct the amount of the bill from his taxes. Legitimate entertainment of clients; prospective customers, or suppliers is, however, a deductible expense.

Real Property—For **tax purposes only** real property may be defined as any asset having a readily established monitary value. This includes real estate, buildings, machinery, tools, vehicles and much, much more. In other contexts real property is defined only as real estate such as homes, farms, etc.

Salvage Value—For income tax purposes, salvage value is understood to mean the remaining worth of an asset after its useful life has terminated.

Self Employment Tax—The payments of self-employed people to the Social Security System.

Short Term Capital Gains—Profits made on the sale or exchange of property and/or assets held less than six months, which are not normally associated with his/her normal line of business. This type of income is treated, for tax purposes, like normal income and is subject to full taxation.

Standard Deduction—The allowable deduction computed by the IRS and figured into their sliding scale charts. These deductions may be fixed as in the case of $1200.00 per dependent, or they may be variable as in the scale tax deduction schedule.

Straight Line Method—A computation method used for determining the amount of interest or depreciation for a one year period on payment amounts that run for more than one year. Although this is by far the easiest method of computation; it is not entirely accurate, since it does not reflect the higher amount of interest charged at the earlier part of the financing of a loan or depreciation. If this method is used throughout the period of a loan, however, it will accurately reflect the interest of the entire loan. For example: $5000.00 is borrowed over a 5 year period at a 9% simple interest rate. The interest is then $450.00, and the total loan is for $5,450.00. Using the straight line method to find the principal plus interest amount for any one year, simply divide $5,450.00 by 5, which equals $1,090.00 per year. To find the interest alone divide $450.00 by 5, which equals $90.00 per year. This same method can be used to figure depreciation. If a building is bought for $80,000.00 and is depreciated over a 15 year period: then by using the straight line method of dividing $80,000.00 by 15 the yearly depreciation is $5,333.33, and by dividing 15 into 100 (the total percent of value), you get a yearly depreciation rate of 6.66%. (Also see depreciation and interest.)

Sum-Of-The-Digits Method—The other (see straight line method) method commonly used to compute interest and/or depreciation. This method gives a more accurate figure on month to month interest, but it is more complicated and therefore more prone to error in calculation. To figure the interest deduction with the sum-of-the-digits method, you first add up all of the payments (not the amounts) but the numbers. For example: payments over 3 years, 36 months, would be added 36 + 35 + 34 + 33 etc. to equal a total of 666. Next, calculate the payments made in that year. For example: 36, 35, 34, 33, 32, 31, 30, 29, 28, and 27 added together equal 315. Then make a fraction of payments made over the total payments, or 315/666. This fraction times the total of interest paid for that period. It can easily be seen that the interest paid during the first 10 months is almost half the total interest for the 3 year loan, and it will be to your advantage to deduct this greater interest during the time you are actually paying it, rather than simply averaging it over the three year period.

Surtax—An extra or additional tax. Specifically, a graduated income tax over and above the usual fixed income tax. This tax is usually levied on the amount by which the net income exceeds a set limit.

Tax Bracket—The level at which each individual taxpayer is taxed, ie: that percentage of his/her taxable income that the IRS claims as tax: 15% of $12,000.00 taxable income. This phrase usually refers to the highest percentage reached.

Taxable Income—The amount of the taxpayer's income actually subject to taxation. That part of the income left after all exemptions and deductions are subtracted.

Tax Loophole—An exception in the tax laws allowing deductions for specific situations and circumstances. These exceptions are usually used by giant corporations to their fullest advantage, but there is no reason the small taxpayer cannot also use these tax exemptions to his/her advantage.

Ten Year Averaging Break—A special long term method of averaging some income, (such as retirement trust benefits) over a 10 year period. (See government form 4792, Chapter 3.)

Vacancy Factor—The percentage used by a property owner or landlord to compute a safety margin into his/her rental charges. For example: a property owner's payments on a house are $2,400.00 per year, his taxes are $400.00 per year, and his repair costs and incidentals are another $40.00 per month. This works out to a cost of $273.33 per month, but since he estimates that the property will be vacant one month in twelve on the average, he must add one-twelfth more to his rental price, or $22.77 more per month. This gives him a base rental price of $296.10 on a break even basis.

Wash Sale—A type of security transaction designated to establish a loss on paper, but resulting in the repurchase of the stock before the legal 30 day minimum limit.

There is one difference between a tax collector and taxidermist . . . the taxidermist leaves the hide . . . [Mortimer Caplan, Director of the Bureau of Internal Revenue, TIME, Feb. 1, 1963]

The art of taxation consists in so plucking the goose as to obtain the largest amount of feathers with the least possible amount of hissing . . . [Attr. J.B. Colbert [1619-1683], Louis XIV's Controller-General of France]

THE FORGOTTEN MAN . . . Who is the Forgotten Man? He is the clean, quiet, virtuous, domestic citizen, who pays his debts and his taxes and is never heard of out of his little circle . . . The Forgotten Man . . . delving away in patient industry, supporting his family, paying his taxes, casting his vote, supporting the church and the school . . . He is the only one for whom there is no provision in the great scramble and the big divide. Such is the Forgotten Man. He works, he votes, generally he prays — but his chief business in life is to pay . . . [W.G. Sumner: THE FORGOTTEN MAN [1883]]